INVENTING THE AXIS OF EVIL

INVENTING THE AXIS OF EVIL

THE TRUTH ABOUT NORTH KOREA, IRAN, AND SYRIA

BRUCE CUMINGS
ERVAND ABRAHAMIAN
MOSHE MA'OZ

THE NEW PRESS

NEW YORK
LONDON

Published in the United States by The New Press, New York, 2004
Distributed by W. W. Norton & Company, Inc., New York

LIBRARY OF CONGRESS CATALOGING-IN-PUBLICATION DATA

Abrahamian, Ervand, 1940-
    Inventing the axis of evil : the truth about North Korea, Iran, and Syria /
Ervand Abrahamian, Bruce Cumings, Moshe Ma'oz.
        p.   cm.
    Includes bibliographical references.
    ISBN 1-56584-904-3
    1. United States—Politics and government—2001-   2. United States—
Foreign relations—Iran.   3. Iran—Foreign relations—United States.
4. United States—Foreign relations—Syria.   5. Syria—Foreign relations—
United States.   6. United States—Foreign relations—Korea (North)
7. Korea (North)—Foreign relations—United States.   8. United States—
Foreign relations—2001-   I. Cumings, Bruce, 1943-   II. Ma'oz, Moshe.
III. Title.

E902.A27 2004
327.730171'82'09045—dc22

                                                                2003068647

The New Press was established in 1990 as a not-for-profit alternative to the
large, commercial publishing houses currently dominating the book publishing
industry. The New Press operates in the public interest rather than for private
gain, and is committed to publishing, in innovative ways, works of educational,
cultural, and community value that are often deemed insufficiently profitable.

The New Press
38 Greene Street, 4th floor
New York, NY 10013
www.thenewpress.com

In the United Kingdom:
6 Salem Road
London W2 4BU

Composition by Westchester Book Composition

Printed in the United States of America

2 4 6 8 10 9 7 5 3 1

CONTENTS

The axis of evil, like the evil empire before it, has already become a lasting cliché of international politics. We learned from the memoirs of David Frum, the former White House speechwriter who coined the now-legendary phrase, how arbitrary that trinity was. Consensus held that three countries sounded better than two, and the unholy conspiracy of Iran, North Korea, and Syria was thus born. It has proven to be a fatal choice as far as Iraq is concerned.

Now that Iraq is under occupation, though, its neighbor Syria is increasingly subject to pressure from the United States. Continuing skirmishes are taking place along the border, and the *New York Times* has reported growing anger in Syria at the number of civilians killed by U.S. soldiers in the border area as well as what are deemed to be provocative overflights by American jet fighters. Iran has, of course, been the subject of constant verbal attacks by Rumsfeld and others in the Bush administration, and the situation in North Korea is so dangerous that no one seems to know what our policy is from one day to the next.

In light of the growing importance of Iran, North Korea, and Syria to Americans and to the world as a whole, we commissioned three leading experts on these countries: Bruce Cumings on North Korea, Ervand Abrahamian on Iran, and Moshe Ma'oz on Syria. We asked each contributor to write an essay, completed in the fall of 2003, that would provide the basic background for each of these countries and also explain U.S. policy toward them over the years. Our contributors worked under particularly difficult circumstances, given the dangerously fluid situation that attains in all three countries, but that very instability makes it all the more crucial to strive to understand these countries, their historical context, and the potential for misunderstanding about them now.

We're very grateful to Cumings, Abrahamian, and Ma'oz for having accepted this challenging but crucial assignment.

André Schiffrin
February 2004

INVENTING THE AXIS OF EVIL

DECOUPLED FROM HISTORY: NORTH KOREA IN THE "AXIS OF EVIL"

Bruce Cumings

> If only it were all so simple! If only there were evil people somewhere, insidiously committing evil deeds, and it were necessary only to separate them from the rest of us and destroy them. But the line dividing good and evil cuts through the heart of every human being.
>
> —Alexander Solzhenitsyn[1]

INTRODUCTION

When George W. Bush listed the Democratic People's Republic of Korea (DPRK) in his "axis of evil" inventory, people who consider themselves knowledgeable typically said one of two things: here's a case of affirmative action for non-Muslims, or a young speechwriter put the infelicitous "axis of anger" into a speech draft, whereupon someone else penciled in the flourish that stuck in the 2002 State of the Union Address. Nothing could be further from the truth. The "axis" fatally conflated three countries that had been contained and deterred for decades with terrorist forces who delight in their anonymity, invisibility, and mocking refusal to take responsibility for the nihilistic mayhem they create. But this wasn't politically correct or inadvertent. The "axis" was deeply reflective of this president's thinking and his affinities for extremists within his administration, reckless adventurers who know nothing about our fractured history with Korea but are sure they are right. In this manner an enduring conflict stretching back to the onset of the Great Depression in which "good and evil" have clashed with shocking abandon was remade and renamed for contemporary American usage.

Kim Sŏng-ju, who took the nom de guerre Kim Il Sung, a man born on the day the *Titanic* sank (April 15, 1912), began his resistance to the forces that initiated the Asian side of the Second World War when he was nineteen years old. The occasion was the euphemistically named "Manchurian incident" in September 1931, when Japanese militarists staged a bombing in search of a provocation that would justify their takeover of China's northeastern provinces. After a swift invasion Tokyo declared these provinces to be *Manchukuo*, the country of the Manchus, a name in search of legitimacy through a link with China's last, failed dynasty (founded by Manchus and known as the Qing, 1644–1911), an absurd proposition that would perhaps occur only to emperor-worshipping Japanese. Henry Pu Yi, the boy-emperor and Roaring Twenties bon vivant, became the figurehead for this puppet state, founded on March 1, 1932. The imperialists chose that date to denigrate the moment in 1919 when Koreans rose up across their country in search of independence, a date sacred to Koreans. Kim Il Sung, who fought fiercely against the imperial occupiers of China and Korea for the next decade in harsh circumstances unimaginable to an American,[2] died in 1994 just after he and Jimmy Carter had accomplished the first major diplomatic breakthrough ever to solve a serious problem between Washington and P'yŏngyang—the Framework Agreement that for the next eight years froze North Korea's massive and expensive complex of nuclear reactors.

American forces landed in Korea in the immediate aftermath of the Pacific War (1931–45), and have never left. On the day after the B-29 nicknamed "Bock's Car" obliterated Nagasaki, John J. McCloy, Lt. Col. Dean Rusk, and Col. Charles H. Bonesteel unilaterally divided this ancient country, consulting no Koreans and no allies, and once U.S. occupation forces arrived three weeks later, they immediately set about repressing the mushrooming progressive movements that spread throughout the peninsula, led by the resistance to Japanese imperialism. Americans sought instead to fashion a pro-American elite from among those who had served Japan.

One of their first acts was to form a "governing commission" of "several hundred conservatives" whom the head of U.S. military intelligence had identified within one week of the Americans landing at Inch'ŏn on September 8, 1945. When Kim Il Sung effectively came to power in the North in February 1946, they refused to have anything to do with him—a nonrecognition policy that is now entering its seventh decade. Four years later Kim commanded the Korean People's Army, led by officers who had fought with him in Manchuria and full of tens of thousands of Korean soldiers who had fought in the Chinese civil war that succeeded the Pacific War. On the southern side in the tumultuous summer of 1949 Kim Sŏk-wŏn commanded the 38th parallel; he had achieved fame in the 1930s after the Japanese promoted his career, which consisted of tracking down and killing prominent Korean and Chinese guerrillas at the behest of Gen. Hideki Tōjō and other leading militarists. Almost the entire officer corps of the South Korean army had a similar provenance.[3] A year later civil war erupted, millions died but the peninsula returned only to the 1953 status quo ante, and today, as for the past half-century, tens of thousands of American soldiers stand on quotidian 24/7 alert against the DPRK. One can only conclude that the American occupation of Korea quickly turned into a manifest failure, an insoluble, never-ending nightmare that drains our blood and treasure: the leadership of North Korea was a problem for the United States sixty years ago,[4] and sixty Septembers later it remains so.

Bush and Son whited all this out. Shortly after the Persian Gulf War ended North Korea emerged as "the next renegade

state," run by "a vicious dictator" with SCUD missiles, a million
men under arms, and "weapons of mass destruction" — in short,
another Iraq.[5] The reigning post–Cold War trope of the "rogue
state" was fastened upon the DPRK instantly and effortlessly, a
sleight-of-hand transference that pretended as if five decades of
conflict and the enormous American responsibility for it, never
existed. Soon Cable News Network and the media more generally
took the first Bush administration's political rhetoric for its own,
never failing to show the soldiers of this "rogue state" marching
in goose-step formation. The "axis of evil" speech recapitulated
this propaganda, but it is not clear that the North took it too
seriously — apart from denouncing Bush for the umpteenth time.
It took another September to cast the die, when the younger
Bush tabled through the National Security Council a new doctrine of preemptive strikes, targeted specifically against Iraq, Iran,
and North Korea. In March 2003 Bush's illegal invasion of Iraq
showed this to be a doctrine of preventive war, but the North
didn't waste time waiting to see the actual implementation of the
"Bush doctrine." From October 2002 onward they acted as if
their only deterrent to this irresponsible administration was a nuclear one, a decision that any general sitting in P'yŏngyang (or
Tehran) would have made. Whether the North Koreans actually
have a nuclear deterrent, and if so whether they can be talked out
of it with the right combination of carrots and sticks, remains to
be seen. But if diplomacy fails and the North emerges as a nuclear
power it will have been a stunning defeat for U.S. strategy, and
history will see it as Bush's bomb.

This insecure, unprepared, unworldly, and un-elected man,
lacking a single distinction before he headed into the Oval Office
that was clearly his own except the elect of his prominent family,
finally found meaning in his life on September 11. It was his Pearl
Harbor, as he has often said, thus achieving another stunning
conflation between an "axis of evil" that had decisively trans-

formed the balance of power in the world by the time the United States got around to joining the war in December 1941, and a bunch of atavistic, nihilistic, adolescent-minded fanatics who think a new Islamic ascendancy can be ushered in if they just kill as many of the infidel as possible, in as many "big bangs" as possible. But Bush's utter lack of a historical sensibility, while not a tragic failing (he has no tragic failings), has hurtled his administration down a path that can have no good outcome. And it gets worse, because Bush believes deeply in his anointed role (not since McKinley seized the Philippines have we had a president who justifies his aggression by virtue of an open pipeline to God), his errant analogies, the straws he grasps at in the winds of unknown history, his pathetic attempts to channel Churchillian rhetoric and gravitas, the very words he gets from experienced ventriloquists like Dick Cheney—history on a bumper sticker or billboard.

I often ask my students if a sense of history makes a difference. Some of them, and all too many Americans, think it does not. Of course it is everything, indispensable, and without it a leader is nothing. Take Bush's analogy with Pearl Harbor. Since September 11 a large billboard has greeted Chicagoans speeding northward on the Kennedy Expressway: "Never forget!" declares the statement in the middle, flanked on the left and right by two dates: December 7, 1941, and September 11, 2001. It is not surprising that the first event Americans would think about after the terrorist attacks was Pearl Harbor, since foreign attacks on American territory had occurred so rarely—essentially two big ones in two centuries, in 1812 and 1941. Using a commercial airliner as a deadly missile also qualified the attack on the Pentagon as an act of war. September 11 has clearly become "a date that will live in infamy," and everyone will remember exactly where he or she was when first seeing or hearing this news. But these facts exhaust the analogies with Pearl Harbor.

Pearl Harbor was a case of unprovoked aggression (Tōjō in command, as in Manchukuo), and has since been condemned not only by Americans but by the best Japanese historians. As Prof. Ienaga Saburo wrote decades ago, Japan's militarists "charged recklessly into an unwinnable war and continued to the point of national destruction."[6] But it was no *more* than military aggression, of a kind the world had experienced many times before; aggression across international boundaries for reasons of state was as common to history before 1941 as it was rare after 1945. Furthermore Japan's attack targeted purely military objectives: total American casualties in the Pearl raid were 2,335 naval, army, and marine personnel dead, 1,143 wounded. Total civilians killed: sixty-eight.[7] The stunning (if Phyrric) strategic success of Japan's operation is frequently remembered, but few recall the precision with which the attack separated soldier and civilian. A counterforce strike against the American fleet, it had a soldier-to-civilian kill ratio of about thirty-four to one.

If a direct attack on the Pacific fleet was unexpected, it still came decades after the first thoughts of war with Japan emerged in Washington. In 1909 U.S. Navy planners chose Pearl Harbor as the chief American base in the Pacific, and a year later the Taft administration began a systematic consideration of conflict with Japan—within months it had worked out a detailed "Orange Plan" for war.[8] December 7, 1941, also came after several years of what Harvard professor Akira Iriye has called a U.S.-Japan Cold War, the U.S. oil embargo (clearly an act of war), and weeks of expecting Japan to strike at American interests. About ten days before Pearl Harbor, Secretary of War Henry Stimson entered in his diary a famous and much-argued statement—that he had met with President Franklin D. Roosevelt to discuss the evidence of impending hostilities with Japan, and the question was "how we should maneuver them [the Japanese] into the position of firing the first shot without allowing too much danger to ourselves."

Stimson later told a Congressional inquiry that it may be dangerous to wait until the enemy "gets the jump on you by taking the initiative;" nonetheless, " . . . in letting the Japanese fire the first shot, we realized that in order to have the full support of the American people it was desirable . . . that there should remain no doubt in anyone's mind as to who were the aggressors."[9]

It is not my purpose to argue that Stimson (or Roosevelt) "maneuvered" Japan (or the United States) into the war, but it is noteworthy that most American wars have begun when "the other guy" fired the first shot. The strategy of passive defense is not innocent of considerations of power, as any psychologist knows; a nation of superior strength will often find advantage in letting the weaker side strike first. This is also the preferred strategy of a line of statesmen that begins with Roosevelt and Stimson. During the Vietnam War his interlocuter for *The Stimson Papers*, McGeorge Bundy, remarked that "Pleikus are like streetcars." When an attack like the one on the U.S. Marine base at Pleiku comes along, you jump on and ride it for what it's worth to you—in his case, to escalate the war. September 11 was Bush's Pleiku, but he got on the wrong streetcar, drove it the wrong way, toward the wrong destination, and quickly rode it into a dead end.

By contrast with Pearl Harbor the attacks on the Twin Towers were utterly unexpected and unprovoked, had no rational military purpose, took an overwhelming number of innocent civilian lives, and lacked the essential relationship between violent means and political ends that, as Clausewitz taught us, must govern any act of war. In its utter recklessness and indifference to consequences, its craven anonymity, and its lack of any discernible "program" save for inchoate revenge, September 11 was an apolitical act. What was the terrorists' next step, what was their strategy, how would the chief terrorists know when they have achieved their goals? In short, these black events will go down in history as acts of catastrophic nihilism—and precisely that terrible quality makes them far more shocking than anything that happened on December 7, 1941.

For all these reasons, Pearl Harbor is a bad analogy with September 11. But it is hardly Bush's alone: a leading liberal commentator, Bill Moyers, wrote in *The Nation* that "In response to the sneak attack on Pearl Harbor, Americans waged and won a great war, then came home to make this country more prosperous and just. It is not beyond this generation to live up to that example."[10] Flawed thinking animates the whole statement: no "great war" unfolded; the enemy was diabolical but cannot remotely be compared to the might and weight of the real axis, Nazi Germany or militarist Japan; millions of Americans are not fighting overseas on several fronts (even if hundreds of thousands are trying to win the peace in the countries we have occupied so thoughtlessly and carelessly); and the current generation is, by definition, no better or worse off than the generation that won victory in World War II (except in the minds of baby-boomer commentators who took rather a long time to comprehend the immense sacrifices that their parents made in the 1940s). Still, Bill Moyers is one of America's best—and most liberal—commentators, which suggests the staying power of this flawed and disturbing analogy.

Perhaps Bush's most foolish statement, however, and one that calls up no analogies among previous American presidents, was his siren song after the "major fighting" ended in Iraq: "Bring 'em on!"[11] And what has he brought on? A military occupation of Iraq that immediately turned into a wretched nightmare, and promises over the long run to be more expensive and difficult than those of South Korea, Japan, or Germany (in spite of the tremendous turmoil in South Korea under the U.S. occupation, I never found evidence that even a single American soldier had been killed in anger by a Korean). This is clearly the worst crisis since the Vietnam War, if not necessarily the "quagmire" that was always a false metaphor for Vietnam (*we* were the problem there, not Vietnamese fighting by any means at their disposal for their national independence in a thirty-years' war). The Iraq war and its aftermath represent a fundamental traducing of the principles of American foreign relations going back to 1941, a lawlessness that began with contempt for our traditional allies, multilateral consultations and action, the tested doctrines of containment and deterrence, and proceeded to violate the United Nations Charter by invading Iraq, making the lawgiver of the postwar world system into a criminal—and thus unleashing into the world from the top, so to speak, the law of the jungle and a host of unforeseen consequences that fall upon all of our heads today. My main concern in this essay is North Korea, but the reader will see that this crisis contains all the elements I have just mentioned, but threatens to be worse than Iraq: it carries a potential for danger not seen since the Cuban Missile Crisis menaced the lives of everyone on earth.

KOREA AND IRAQ: HOW THE UNITED STATES FARES IN OCCUPYING AN UNRULY COUNTRY

One of the more meaningless statements about history is the one most often cited: Santayana's "those who forget history are condemned to repeat it." If that were true, this ahistorical country would be refighting the revolutionary and civil wars every few generations. Basically there are four possibilities: people can forget history and repeat it (Santayana is right, it does happen, and Americans are especially vulnerable); or they can forget it but not repeat it (the usual outcome); or they can remember and repeat (this is what the two Bushes did: Bush the Elder wanted to use the Gulf War to "put Vietnam behind us" but failed, while his son fancies himself post–Pearl Harbor while up to his gills in Middle East and South Asian mayhem); or they can remember and not repeat (Santayana's preference). Obviously the better question is, what history are we choosing to remember (or forget)? My life has taught me that the best purchase on the meaning of our history since 1941 is the coinage put down by the first-team squad of British and American foreign policy makers. Churchill wrote the history of World War II in several august volumes, but at least he had the decency to say that history would treat him kindly because he would write it. In 1947 Stimson called upon himself to say in *Harper's* that Truman was right to drop the atomic bombs, because that act saved millions of lives. In 1954 Dean Acheson stepped up to the plate to tell us what the Korean War meant, and his words and the book he subsequently wrote on the subject still hold sway: the first war, the war in the summer of 1950 for containment, saved the day and was the finest hour of the Truman presidency; the second war that broke out when we sought to liberate North Korea was a debacle that destroyed the Truman administration. But this didn't happen to him—it happened to Douglas MacArthur. Acheson thus squares the circle, and a long list of historians merely follow in his wake. John J. McCloy gave us what happened in the occupation of Germany, Henry Kissinger gives us the tragedy of Vietnam, and Arthur Schlesinger Jr. (only briefly a statesman) begets the consensus on everything since the Mayflower docked. The result? Herculean efforts are required to figure out what has actually happened in the world since 1945.

Most Americans seem unaware of it, but the United States occupied southern Korea in 1945, set up a three-year military government, moved into the Yongsan military base in Seoul that the Japanese built in 1894, and ensconced the commander—Gen. John R. Hodge—in the executive mansion of the Japanese governor-general, otherwise known as the "Blue House" (successive Korean presidents also occupied it until it was finally torn down in the 1990s). The Americans ruled from the Government-General building, a stately beaux arts masterpiece designed by a German architect but installed by the Japanese at an angle precise enough to destroy the centuries-old geomancy of the royal palaces that sit on the same ground. (From above, the building was configured to look like the Chinese character for the sun, as in *Nippon* and "rising sun"). The high command—except for Hodge—billeted in the Chosen (Korea) and Hanto (Peninsula) hotels that the Japanese built, quickly renamed the Choson and the Bando; for decades the U.S. embassy sat across the street from the Bando, ensconced in a building owned by the Mitsui *zaibatsu* group before 1945.

Hodge and his staff ruled through the modern, penetrative state bureaucracy that the Japanese also built, and filled out the administration with civil affairs officers trained for military government in Japan. Since MacArthur never set one up, Korea essentially got the occupation designed for Japan—an irony only slightly less vexing than that this country, unified for a millennium, also got divided. This was an absolute injustice, since Korea was the first victim of Japanese aggression in 1910 when it was colonized. But MacArthur and leaders in Washington wanted a unified Japan presided over by a unilateral administration that paid mere lip service to our allies, preserving American freedom of action which could then be used to revive and rebuild Japan as the centerpiece of U.S. strategy in East Asia—and subsequently a workshop for the world. Soon hundreds of American military bases dotted Japan and Korea, most of which remain today. (Yongsan now sits in the middle of a city of 11 million, home to one-third of the South Korean population; the Pentagon finally wants to give the base back, mainly because it has become fly-paper for innumerable daily protests by Koreans outside the gates.) Thus began the unilateral, heavily militarized tendency in postwar American foreign policy toward East and Southeast Asia, an empire that finds its expression in an extensive and seemingly permanent archipelago of military bases. Bush merely redirected this Asian strategy to the rest of the world.

John Reed Hodge, a war hero often called "the Patton of the Pacific" and a key commander in the bloodiest Pacific battle of them all for Okinawa, got the nod for occupation duty because his XXIV Corps was the closest substantial force to Korea. The Corps' embarkation date was moved up three times owing to high-level fears of Soviet expansion and Korean guerrillas supposedly flooding in from Manchuria, and because of Japanese worries about "Communists" and "independence agitators" trying to take advantage of the vacuum of power inside Korea. On August 29 the colonial Government-General radioed to Okinawa that

> local Japanese authorities eagerly await the arrival of the Allied Forces . . . and urgently desire that the Allied forces will fully take into consideration the actual conditions on the sport before proceeding with the disarmament of Japanese forces and the transfer of administrative organs from the Japanese hand.

Hodge hearkened to this Japanese propaganda, later using it to justify "that scramble move" from Okinawa to Seoul.[12] Soon America's "black ships" arrived in Inch'ŏn harbor, and Korea began the most anomalous period in its history since 668 A.D.: the era of national division.

In my classes I struggle to get students to understand that there is no such thing as objectivity or even-handedness in such a situation, even though that is what the laws of warfare and post-warfare called for at the time, in cases of a "pacific" (i.e., peaceable) military occupation. Every hour, every day, Americans had to make decisions about whom to hire, whom to fire, and what to do. But it may be that our contemporary occupation of Iraq, unfolding under the 24/7 gaze of television, can be a mnemonic to re-experience that lost past in the unfolding present.

On September 8, 1945, U.S. combat troops first occupied Korea; three months later Hodge "declared war" on the Communists (the ones in the southern zone; he mistook a mélange of leftists, anticolonial resisters, populists, and advocates of land reform for "Communists"), and in the spring of 1946 he issued his first warning to Washington of an impending North Korean invasion. If our contemporary occupation of Iraq follows suit, the country will be divided (probably into three parts, not two), five years later a civil war will erupt and millions will die but nothing will be solved; and in the 2060s, nearly 40,000 American troops will still be there, holding the line against the evil enemy (whoever he might be), with a new war possible at any moment. The Iraq occupation cost $4 billion per month in 2003; for comparison, the estimated direct and indirect cost of maintaining the American security commitment to South Korea and myriad military bases, runs from $17 billion to $42 billion annually, depending on how the costs are calculated.[13]

The U.S. military command, along with high-ranking emissaries dispatched from Washington like John J. McCloy, tended to interpret resistance to U.S. desires in the South as radical and pro-Soviet. In particular, the United States saw the "People's Republic" that had emerged in early September throughout the South as part of a Soviet master plan to dominate all of Korea. Radical activity, like ousting landlords and attacking Koreans in the colonial police, was usually a matter of settling scores left over from the colonial period, or of demands by Koreans to run their own affairs. But it immediately became wrapped up with Soviet-American rivalry, such that the Cold War arrived in Korea in the last months of 1945. Within one week of their arrival, Americans in Seoul who had never met a Korean and knew nothing of this ancient civilization decided that they knew which Korean political leaders were best. That pool of several hundred held most of the leaders who would subsequently shape South Korean politics. Had we not supported them with military force, many would have called an end to their colonial service and exiled themselves to Japan.

We can trace this rapid transformation in the daily reports of Colonel Nist regarding the conversations and interviews that he and other officers held with Koreans in the Bando Hotel. By September 15 Nist's judgments were embodied in a report that H. Merrell Benninghoff, State Department political advisor to General Hodge, sent back to Washington:

> Southern Korea can best be described as a powder keg ready to explode at the application of a spark.

> There is great disappointment that immediate independence and sweeping out of the Japanese did not eventuate.

> [Those Koreans who] achieved high rank under the Japanese are considered pro-Japanese and are hated almost as much as their masters. . . .

> All groups seem to have the common idea of seizing Japanese property, ejecting the Japanese from Korea, and achieving immediate independence. Beyond this they have few ideas.

> Korea is completely ripe for agitators. . . .

> The most encouraging single factor in the political situation is the presence in Seoul of *several hundred con-*

servatives among the older and better educated
Koreans. Although many of them have served the Japanese, that stigma ought eventually to disappear . . .
although they may not constitute a majority they are
probably the largest single group.[14]

Not bad for a week's work. Americans with nary a whit of
knowledge about Korean history and civilization reached out to
those they could talk to, people wealthy enough to have studied
English during the Japanese period, and proclaimed them liberals
and democrats. Within days the United States had also helped to
organize the Korean Democratic Party (a forerunner of the Liberal Democratic Party organized in Japan in 1955 with much help
and funds from the CIA), a party that structured the so-called
opposition down to Kim Dae Jung's election in 1998 — an election
that represented the first real transition from the regime and the
elites that Americans sponsored during the occupation. Even
more notorious collaborators like Pak Hŭng-sik, an industrialist
who built airplane parts for Japan's fighters during the Pacific
War, tossed a lot of money around and quickly became favorites
of the American command.

The problem was that Korean society had no base for either
a liberal or a democratic party as Americans understood it; the
vast majority of the population were poor peasants, and a tiny
minority held most of the wealth: landowners who traced their
genealogies and their landholdings back centuries constituted the
base of the KDP. They were the elite of Korean society before
and during the colonial period, but by 1945 nearly all of them
were widely perceived to have fattened under colonial rule while
everybody else suffered. The evidence could not be more clear:
the United States intervened on behalf of the smallest group in
Korea, not Nist's "largest single group," and helped to perpetuate
their privileges thereafter.

The collaborationist taint of the anointed hundreds and their allies led Hodge to seek a patriotic figurehead—a Chalabi. The Office of Strategic Services (OSS, forerunner of the CIA) found their man in Syngman Rhee, an exiled politician who had haunted and annoyed Foggy Bottom for decades. He was hustled aboard a military transport over State Department objections, flown to Tokyo where he met secretly with MacArthur, and then flown into Korea on the *Bataan* (MacArthur's personal plane), on October 16, 1945. Four days later General Hodge introduced him to the Korean public and Rhee proclaimed himself the father of the country. This Chalabi arrived courtesy of M. Preston Goodfellow, who had been deputy director of the OSS under William "Wild Bill" Donovan; later on he played an important but still murky role in the outbreak of warfare in 1950. Goodfellow then, like Donald Rumsfeld and Paul Wolfowitz in the Bush administration in 2003, thought Rhee (or Chalabi) had more of "the American point of view" than other Korean (or Iraqi) leaders, and made the arrangements to deposit him back in Korea. Goodfellow then arrived in Korea himself, seeking to set up a separate, anticommunist southern government. He was forced to leave Korea in May 1946 when information surfaced that Rhee had promised him a concession on wealthy Korean gold mines (which happened to be in the North).

In October 1945, as it happened, both the American and the Soviet military commands sponsored welcoming ceremonies for two returned exiles: on October 20 Rhee was allowed to give a strongly anticommunist speech with Hodge sitting at his side, and Soviet officers stood behind Kim Il Sung, introduced in P'yŏngyang as a hero of the resistance to Japan on October 14, 1945. Did a Soviet "Goodfellow" deposit Kim back in P'yŏngyang? Not so. Original research in five languages by Prof. Wada Haruki found that just before the Manchurian guerrillas returned to Korea, the top leaders agreed among themselves to promote Kim Il Sung as the maximum figure, for reasons that included his wider reputation and his personal force and charisma.[15] Along with other Manchurian guerrillas they became the core of the North Korean hierarchy down to the late 1990s (of forty top leaders in 1998, only one was under sixty: Kim Jong Il).

The State Department frequently objected to favoring one Korean group over another, but John J. McCloy visited Korea in November 1945 and sided with Hodge, saying that if the United States did not "build up on our own a reasonable and respected government or group of advisors," Communists would seize the government instead.[16] By the third week of November Hodge and his advisors had come up with a plan for a "governing commission" to be formed by Koreans at Hodge's direction, which would quickly integrate with the U.S. military government and, soon thereafter, succeed it (with Hodge retaining veto power over its activities). As for the Russians, they would be "informed in advance" and encouraged to send people to join the commission, "but if Russian participation is not forthcoming plans should be carried out for Korea south of 38th parallel." The person who wrote this memo, William Langdon (another State Department advisor to Hodge, but one with considerable experience in pre-1945 Korea) thought that a southern government thus constituted would be good for foreign interests:

> The old native regime internally was feudal and corrupt but the record shows that it was the best disposed toward foreign interests of the three Far Eastern nations, protecting foreign lives and property and enterprises and respecting treaties and franchises. I am sure that we may count on at least as much from a native government evolved as above. . . . [17]

The "governing commission" turned into something called the Representative Democratic Council, which Syngman Rhee soon dominated. An American advisor who informed himself deeply on Korean politics, subsequently remarked that this body "was neither democratic, nor representative, nor did it ever counsel." But Rhee was a wily and tough politician who understood Americans and their deep, unthinking, and uninformed anticommunism, and made that his stock in trade from his arrival in 1945 until 1960 when the Korean people threw him out. By 1949, when he personally chose Kim Sŏk-wŏn to command the 38th parallel, he had 100,000 political prisoners in his jails.

Hodge worried most about the political, social, and economic disorder that was everywhere around him. Against direct orders from the State Department, in December 1945 he began forming a native Korean army. First came an English-language school for the Japanese-speaking Koreans who had served the empire, and then a military academy that later graduated all of the ROK's plotters of the first military coup in 1961 (led by the 8th class) and the subsequent military coup in 1980 (class of '55). In the fall of 1946, the second class of graduates included Park Chung Hee, who made the first coup, and Kim Chae-gyu, the head of Korean central intelligence who murdered him over dinner one night in 1979. By the time the invasion came in 1950, the South Korean state was essentially the colonial state in mildly altered form, with the 100,000-strong army and the very large paramilitary National Police led almost entirely by officers who had served the Japanese. For that reason Hodge needed some political cover, adopting a "Koreanization" plan in November 1945 to go along with his "governing commission." Ring any Iraqi bells?

Once the American occupation chose to bolster the status quo and resist a thorough reform of colonial legacies, it immediately ran into monumental opposition from the mass of South Koreans. Most of the first year of the occupation, 1945–46, was given over to suppression of many people's committees, labor organizations, and peasant unions that had emerged in the provinces. This provoked a massive rebellion that spread over four provinces in the fall of 1946; after it was suppressed, radical activists developed a significant guerrilla movement in 1948 and 1949, and touched off another major uprising at the port of Yŏsu in October 1948. Much of this disorder owed to the unresolved land problem, as conservative landlords used their central bureaucratic power to block redistribution of land to peasant tenants. The North Koreans of course tried to take advantage of this discontent, but unimpeachable internal evidence shows that nearly all of the dissidents and guerrillas were southerners, upset about southern policies. Indeed, the left wing's strength was in those provinces most removed from the 38th parallel, in the southwestern Chŏllas which historically had been rebellious, and in the southeastern Kyŏngsang provinces, which had felt the greatest impact from Japanese colonialism. Hodge liked such people because all the alternatives seemed worse, especially any political group thought to be left of center (as an American would define it).

Roger Baldwin, for many years the head of the American Civil Liberties Union, toured Korea in May 1947. "The country is literally in the grip of a police regime and a private terror," he wrote to friends; "you get the general impression of a beaten, discouraged people." He saw a prison where 1,000 people were held for organizing labor unions and strikes. Koreans "want all foreigners to get out and let them build their nation." Were the Americans to pull out, however, he thought that a civil war would result. But after the American G-2 (intelligence) chief showed him political reports on the countryside, Baldwin concluded that "a state of undeclared war" already existed in Korea. Korean leaders told him that the government was "full of Quislings" and "toadies to the Americans," but it was the American retention of the hated colonial police, one of them thought, that was the key to the "present chaos."[18]

General Hodge wrote a remarkable report after the first three months of occupation, presenting a situation that paralleled the mess in Iraq after "the end of major fighting":[19]

> [There] is growing resentment against all Americans in the area including passive resistance. . . . Every day of drifting under this situation makes our position in Korea more untenable and decreases our waning popularity. . . . The word pro-American is being added to pro-Jap, national traitor, and collaborator.

If by "occidental standards Koreans are not ready for independence," they nonetheless want their independence immediately. Were this to happen, Hodge thought southern Korea would be "extremely fertile ground for the establishment of Communism":

> The approximate international influences and our occupation policies of insuring all freedom and maintaining property rights and order among liberated oriental people favor communistic activities.
>
> Koreans well know that the Russians have a force locally of about 4 to 1 to Americans and with the usual oriental slant are willing to do homage and are doing homage to the man with the largest weapon. On the part of the masses there is an increasing tendency to look to Russia for the future.
>
> In summary, the U.S. occupation of Korea . . . is surely drifting to the edge of a political-economic abyss from which it can never be retrieved with any credit to United States prestige in the Far East. Positive action on the international level or the seizure of

complete initiative in South Korea by the U.S. in the very near future is absolutely essential to stop this drift.

If no "positive action" were to follow upon his report, then Hodge urged instead a mutual withdrawal of U.S. and Russian forces from Korea, thus to "leave Korea to its own devices and an inevitable internal upheaval for its own self-purification."

With sixty years of hindsight—or even five, in 1950—we can imagine a cauterizing fire that would have settled Korea's multitude of social and political problems caused by four decades of brutal colonial rule and instant "liberation," a purifying upheaval that might have been pretty awful, but nothing like the millions of lives lost in 1950–53, or the thousands in the April revolution of 1960, or the Kwangju rebellion of 1980—or the crisis today, which again threatens the lives of millions. Had the Americans and the Russians quit Korea, a leftist regime would have taken over quickly, a revolutionary nationalist government which, over time, would have moderated and rejoined the world community—as did China, as has Vietnam today. But we have to imagine this because Americans do not understand the point of social revolutions, never having had one themselves; to allow this to happen would have meant Hodge and lots of other Americans would have occupied Korea only to "turn it over to the Communists." Indeed, this is exactly what Harry Truman's friend, Edwin Pauley, told the president in an important report after his tour of Korea in May 1946:

> Communism in Korea could get off to a better start than practically anywhere else in the world. The Japanese owned the railroads, all of the public utilities including power and light, as well as all of the major industries and natural resources. Therefore, if these

are suddenly found to be owned by "The People's Committee" [The Communist Party], they will have acquired them without any struggle of any kind or any work in developing them. This is one of the reasons why the U.S. should not waive its title or claim to Japanese external assets located in Korea until a democratic [capitalistic] form of government is assured.[20]

The Americans would not turn Korea over to the Koreans, and so they got on with the "positive action" necessary to create an anticommunist South Korea. Korea thus became a harbinger of policies later followed throughout the world—in Greece, Indochina, Iran, Guatemala, Cuba, Nicaragua—where Americans came to defend anyone calling themselves anticommunist, because the alternative was always thought to be worse. And six decades later, the Korean problem remains unsolved.

General Hodge eventually came to understand what Korean political conditions were really like (and to loathe Syngman Rhee), as opposed to the knee-jerk reactions of Colonel Nist in September 1945. In late 1947 he captured in his homespun way the essence of the American dilemma, as it fluctuated between the unhappy poles of supporting people whose one virtue was anticommunism and opposing native leftists, while hoping for a liberal outcome for which Korean society had no base:

We always have the danger of Fascism taking over when you try to fight Communism. It is a very difficult political situation that we run into. Germany was built up by Hitler to fight Communism, and it went to Nazism. Spain the same thing. On the other hand, when the Communists build up—when Communism builds up—democracy is crushed, and the

nation goes Communist. Now, what is the answer on
the thing? How in the dickens are you going to get
political-in-the-middle-of-the-road out of the mess.
Just bring[ing] it up for discussion. I don't know the
answer. I wish I did.

There was no middle in Korea, thanks to the Japanese, and there
would not be until the 1980s.

After the civil war ended the southern leaders and their coun-
terparts in the North set about erecting impenetrable barriers to
any kind of contact between their countrymen on either side of
the DMZ, thus institutionalizing the thoroughly divided two Korean states that are now in their second half-century. Roy Andrew
Grinker's recent book is a strong argument for the quintessential
characteristic of the two Koreas today *being* their separation, their
division from each other, the "division systems" that have been
built up over decades, and ideals of unification invoked by both
sides in ways that are simultaneously utopian and unreachable.
Thus the half-century-old division and the impossible dream of
unification are both constitutive of what it means to be Korean
today, and more generally, "what it means to live in the mod-
ernist age of provisional truths and homelands."[21]

American leaders have never understood the North Korea that
emerged from this cauldron of conflict and war. Their "intelligence failure" is not their failure to penetrate and spy on the
North, even though they have failed miserably in that effort, too;
it is their failure to grasp who these people are, where they came
from, and what they want. This is the subject of my recent book,
but here I would just like to retrieve a contretemps that occurred
when Soviet premier Alexei Kosygin and the head of the KGB,
Yuri Andropov, journeyed to P'yŏngyang in 1965 in search of
reconciliation after the North had sided with China in the Sino-
Soviet split and had come out four-square for the "Juche" ide-

ology of self-reliance and autarky. Instead they caught hell from
Kim Il Sung (see my italics).[22]

> Comrade Kosygin again assured [Kim] that the USSR
> takes the support of the DPRK's foreign policy as that
> of its own. In explaining USSR foreign policy, Com-
> rade Kosygin said that until the October Plenum of
> the CC CPSU, much subjective influence of Khru-
> shchev, which the Central Committee of the USSR
> disapproved of, had also penetrated into this area of
> CPSU policy. Comrade Kim Il Sung interrupted with
> the remark: *"Of course, we even thought that he would
> go to the FRG to see Erhard in order to sell out the GDR*
> [East Germany]."
>
> Comrade Kosygin did not react to this remark and
> continued. He said that in every country there are
> many peculiarities, especially national ones. Khru-
> shchev showed no interest in taking these peculiarities
> into consideration. *You have been accusing us of many
> things.* Although your own reservations were small
> and concerned mainly economic problems, you en-
> dorsed and emphasized many of the Chinese accusa-
> tions." *Kim Il Sung reacted by pointing out that the
> KWP line had always been independent and not Chinese.*
> "We always stood," he said, "and will always stand for
> pure Marxism-Leninism without any admixtures" and
> repeated that *"we implement the purest Marxism and
> condemn as false both the Chinese admixtures and the
> errors of the CPSU."*
>
> [Kosygin]: *"You have been accusing us of not fighting
> against imperialism and that we even collude with it.* Do
> you really think that we, of all people, would be ca-

pable of colluding with the imperialists against communist parties?"

Here again Kim Il Sung intervened with the remark that Khrushchev supposedly was cozying up to Eisenhower and Kennedy. Comrade Kosygin replied by pointing out that *it is not dignified to make such remarks* at a meeting at this level.

In further discussion, Comrade Kosygin informed the KWP leadership in detail about the USSR's assistance to the national liberation struggle and the preparation of guerrilla units in the USSR and asked of Kim Il Sung: "Could [you] possibly write about this in the newspapers? *And you have been trumpeting to the world that we are doing nothing.*" Comrade Kim Il Sung reacted to that as follows: "*OK, so finally you have been publishing strong articles against imperialism in* Pravda," to which Comrade Kosygin said: "Didn't I tell you that writing in newspapers and hurling insults is far from sufficient anymore? So tell me which of the two methods of helping the national liberation struggle is more effective?" Comrade Kim Il Sung did not answer that.

"*We have often been accused of nationalism,*" [Kim said], "in implementing the slogan regarding the development of our economy. I can assure you that the slogan [Juche] about relying on our own forces has been coined first of all for South Korea. Just look, in South Korea the population is being taught that without the Americans one cannot build the economy. But what have the Americans built there during the past twenty years? Nothing besides airfields and bases. So our slogan has been helping to open the eyes, espe-

cially of the South Korean intellectuals. It shows that
the DPRK is already standing firmly on its own feet.
*You have helped us to stand on our feet. Thank you for
that. But now we are able to walk by ourselves.*" To com-
plement Comrade Kim Il Sung, Foreign Minister Pak
Song-ch'ŏl interjected that it was also thanks to China
that the DPRK is standing on its own feet. *Kim Il
Sung ignored him* and continued: "We start from the
assumption that this slogan is serving our common
cause, including that of the African and Asian countries. They especially are realizing that even a small
country is capable of building its own economy." *You
have also unjustly accused us of nationalism, autarky and
isolation.*

Comrade Kosygin remarked: "The slogan is not
the issue. The slogan could be right. But one must be
able to see that the unification of our forces is what
is important at the present time to help our cause advance faster and better." To this Kim Il Sung [re-
plied]: "With us it is different." Kosygin: "Sure. It's
your own business. But together we could walk better
and faster."

[Kim]: "So do understand our position. We are
connected both with you and with China, both politically and economically. *But this does not mean that we
are going to submit to anyone,* this is what we keep
stressing in our Politburo. Apart from that, we know
that the behavior of our representatives at various international conferences and meetings contradicted this
line. *For that, both we and you bear full responsibility.* In
Khrushchev's time, however, we could hardly proceed
otherwise. He was very unstable. He kept changing

his views like dirty laundry. In the morning, he had a different opinion than in the evening.

"*It's good that you have burned all of Khrushchev's books. There was nothing good in them anyway.* And you are rightly correcting the errors in agriculture caused by Khrushchev. We are grateful that in foreign policy you have been helping the DRV, Cuba and all our countries [of the socialist camp]. As I have already said, *there were rumors that Khrushchev wanted to sell the GDR to Erhard.*

Kosygin: "Calling the discussions is not a question of pride." Kim Il Sung: "But these are discussions called by Khrushchev. You have to understand us. If China doesn't go, neither we nor the Vietnamese can. *You should rather come and fight against imperialism* and we are not going to meddle in other questions. We want to strengthen the relations between the KWP and the CPSU." This ended Kim Il Sung's statement.

Comrade Kosygin thanked him for the sincere information and clarification of the KWP's position and said that he believed the KWP's policy is its own business. Life will show whether it has been correct.

According to Comrade Moskovsky, the impression he gained from the negotiations between Comrades Kosygin and Andropov with Kim Il Sung was that Kim Il Sung showed unusual interest in the evaluation of the current situation in South Vietnam. Even outside the negotiations, *he asked several times with great trepidation* about the views of the Soviet comrades about whether the current events in Southeast Asia might not lead to a "major war."

TO RID THE WORLD OF EVIL: THE BUSH
DOCTRINE AND THE MATRIX OF
AMERICAN FOREIGN POLICY

Ever since Mikhail Gorbachev chose not to mobilize massive Soviet armies on the soil of East Germany and other Communist
states to save them from their own people, thus sealing the fate
of the Soviet empire and bestowing a virtually bloodless victory
on George Kennan's containment doctrine, analysts and pundits
have been vying to define the post–Cold War era, and incidentally
to become the next Kennan: the end of history, back to the future, a clash of civilizations, Jihad vs. McWorld, "the Lexus and
the Olive Tree." But the cunning of history dashed their ambitions and gave us instead an unexpectedly muscle-bound and imperial "Mr. X": George W. Bush. No passive containment or
pusillanimous deterrence for His Accidency: under the National
Security doctrine released in September 2002 we got preemptive
attacks, "counterproliferation" for everyone (except ourselves and
our allies), untold billions for the Pentagon to dissuade any and
all comers from "a military build-up in hopes of surpassing, or
equaling, the power of the U.S.," and endless wars into the dis-
appearing and newly darkening future to "rid the world of evil."[23]
Shortly after the doctrine was announced, NSC director Con-
doleeza Rice sought to calm unnerved allies by saying that preemptive attacks are fine for the United States, but other nations
"should [not] use preemption as a pretext for aggression."[24] Preemption, Ms. Rice opined, is "anticipatory self-defense," that is,
"the right of the United States to attack a country that *it thinks*
could attack it first" (emphasis added).[25] In a sense she was right:
Bush did not use preemption in self-defense; instead he launched
a preventive war to topple the Iraqi regime.

This president who lost the 2000 election by half a million

votes but acted as if he had a mandate, chose to posit his reck-
oning with evil on the post–September 11 "war on terrorism,"[26]
but located instead his Dad's old nemesis: Saddam was hiding
"weapons of mass destruction" and giving the runaround to
United Nations inspectors. Therefore, against the UN Security
Council, our traditional allies (except for Britain), world opinion,
and a significant American minority, Bush launched a war that
appeared to go quickly to its conclusion. Lost in the instant
claims of victory was the illegality of this war, violating the UN
Charter and every precept of war-making by previous presidents
going back 150 years. From Polk's attack on Mexico to the
South's shelling of Fort Sumter, the sinking of the *Maine* and
the *Luisitania,* Pearl Harbor, the Korean War, the Tonkin Gulf
incident, and Iraq's invasion of Kuwait, presidents who were bent
on war or not, expecting it to erupt or not, nonetheless waited
until the enemy made the first move. In the months leading up
to the war Saddam Hussein was almost catatonic in his conspic-
uous desire not to provoke Bush, but the war came anyway—
without provocation and without any reasonable threat that Saddam might attack someone else. In unprecedented fashion Bush
launched a massive war when he could not know what the consequences of that war would be.

Bush's new doctrine was not just about foreign policy, however; it was also about domestic politics and a Republican administration both motivated and flummoxed by deeper conflicts
that go to the heart of this party and its historic foreign policy
stance. This was the first Republican administration truly to em-
body the Republican Right's foreign policy views on a host of
issues: arms control, the environment, the United Nations,
post-Soviet Russia, China, North Korea, Iraq, and the presumed
failings of our traditional European allies. The preemptive doctrine embodied phrases and nuances that had been the stock-in-
trade of right-wing pundits like William Kristol and Charles

Krauthammer, who have long called for a new American imperialism. But there was also a back-to-the-future quality; it recalled
the onset of the Cold War, and the formidable critique of containment by Republicans like James Burnham, co-founder with
William Buckley of the *National Review*.

James Burnham was a former Trotskyite from a wealthy Chicago family, known for his brilliant intellect both at Princeton
and in his 1930s Marxist writings. Later he produced an influential book, *The Managerial Revolution*, celebrating bureaucratic
modernism and his decoupling from Marx and the Left. He subsequently became for the doctrine of liberation or rollback what
Kennan had been for containment: its theorist, its champion, its
Zvengali. Burnham's thought decisively rejected interwar isolationism and provided a bureaucratic rationale for the emerging
national security state, thus bridging the obsolescent isolationists
and the sunbelt, defense budget–hungry Republican Right.
Burnham thus became the intellectual architect of a historic
compromise, between the nativist expansionism of the nine-
teenth century and what ultimately became a stable Cold War
containment system.

Like Bush, Burnham assumed that "the unparalleled strength"
of the American military would continue into the indefinite future and should be maintained against all comers, thereby turning
a merely temporary advantage in global power into a permanent
condition. In 1947 the United States had an exclusive monopoly
on the ultimate weapon, the atomic bomb, and this monopoly
should be used—the bomb "makes politically possible . . . the
domination of the world by a single sufficiently large state."
World empire was to be the goal and atomic weapons the means
in the "Third World War," which Burnham thought had already
begun. "In the creation of this Empire," he wrote, "there would
necessarily be involved the reduction of Communism to impo-

tence," at home and abroad. Within two years, of course, the Soviets detonated their own atomic bomb.

The Struggle for the World appeared just as the Truman Doctrine won favor in the spring of 1947, yet typically Burnham was already moving beyond containment. He thought that by this time the United States was "committed everywhere, on every continent," such that it "can never again withdraw" to a fortress America. Yet the United States was immature, possessing the resources for global power, to be sure, with a distinctly provincial and outmoded world view. He perceptively likened the United States and the USSR to "two mighty, semi-barbarian super-states of the periphery," now dividing the globe between them: "One of the two power centers is itself a child, a border area, of Western civilization. . . . The U.S., crude, awkward, semi-barbarian, nevertheless enters this irreconcilable conflict as the representative of Western culture."

Burnham located three tendencies in American foreign policy. First was the internationalist view, which he thought represented appeasement and error. Next was the isolationist view, placing centrality on the conquest of the American internal market and frontier, but which had now become "distorted and degraded by the inexorable pressure of a historical reality in which they can have no natural outlet," an eloquent and accurate comment. Isolationism was belligerently nationalist and purely unilateralist ("it refuses to intervene responsibly"). What was the third tendency? It would be a mix of containment and liberation, premised upon the immanent reality of an American imperium. Instead of world government or isolationist withdrawal and self-containment, the United States should pursue a "world empire." Such an empire was and would be established "at least partly through force and the threat of force."

An important beginning had been made with the Truman

Doctrine and the containment thesis, Burnham thought, which established a defensive position holding back Soviet expansionism. But such a strategy left unresolved "the problems which generate the crisis in world politics." Instead, the Soviet thrust to empire should be reversed, "turning the[ir] expansive advance into a demoralizing retreat." He therefore recommended that "the defensive policy" (containment) be merged with the "offensive policy," thus to undermine Communist power "in East Europe, northern Iran, Afghanistan, Manchuria, northern Korea and China." Never one to mince words, at the end of the book he pointed to the ultimate objective: "the policy aims not at the defeat of Russia, but at its liberation." *Time* and *Life* magazines gave the Henry Luce imprimatur to the book, with the latter running a condensation. Arthur Schlesinger Jr. was impressed: Burnham might not make a good secretary of state, he wrote, but nonetheless Schlesinger preferred his thesis to the "confusion and messy arguments of the appeasers."[27] Still, Burnham was on the sidelines in 1947, his influence miniscule compared to, say, the architect of containment, George Kennan.

By 1950 a reversal had occurred, with Kennan's influence waning and Burnham's waxing. In *The Coming Defeat of Communism*, published with great Henry Luce fanfare in early 1950, he argued forcefully for rollback. Containment was "too defensive"; it could never be "more than a partial and temporary expedient." The United States faced a "dynamic enemy" on all world fronts. The only answer to this was "the turn to the offensive." Burnham and his friend William F. Buckley Jr. had intelligence connections and seemed well aware of internal shifts going on within the Truman administration, yielding more weight to those who favored "positive action."[28] Burnham was also aware of the ongoing deliberations over NSC 68, the most important of all Cold War documents, saying that "a plan of military re-armament and development is at present going forward." Perhaps more important, in discussing resistance and rollback strategies, he turned first to Albania, which had already been subject to various covert Bay of Pigs–style rollback attempts, each of them about as successful as the Cuban venture but highly secret at the time (and since). He argued for support of Chiang Kai-shek in his resistance to communism, which at an appropriate point "will be able to join the offensive . . . when the wheel enters another cycle," thus to "throw the Communists back out of China."

This second book had far more influence than the earlier one. Burnham's arguments fell on willing ears in the early months of 1950. In late January, a top-secret account of State Department discussions with unnamed senators indicated that several were ready to fight: they said their constituents would "back to the hilt" a preventive war, even if the Soviets had taken no overt action against the United States. One was quoted as saying, "why don't we get into this thing now and get it over with before the time is too late?"[29] R.A. Wormser, a member of a Wall Street committee on foreign policy, wrote to "Wild Bill" Donovan, A.A. Berle, Joseph L. Broderick, and others on the same committee in February 1950 that "the appearance of Burnham's book coincidental with the creation of our subcommittee is encouraging." Wormser thought the peace settlement had been too punitive on Germany and Japan. He argued for a united Germany, a restoration of "the eastern borders," and a general offensive against the Soviets:

> Surprise after surprise, blow after blow, attack after attack. In every geographical area and in every political and economic and social area. Energies spent on defense and blocking are lost to the offense, and we cannot only contain Russia, but [must] drive her back.

The United States had simply been "waiting always for their next move," and while "there are limits," morality must give way to realism. Thus, the members should prepare a list of Cold War strategies and tactics — "including everything we can think of, however extreme."[30] In March 1950 Robert Lovett, enormously influential and a charter "wise man," referred to "the war in which we are presently engaged" and said, "we should fight with no holds barred."

> We should find every weak spot in the enemy's armor, both on the periphery and at the center, and hit him with anything that comes to hand. Anything we do short of an all-out effort is inexcusable. We should cause them trouble wherever we can. There are plenty of partisans and dissidents on the enemy's borders and within his camp who are willing to fight . . . if we give them some leadership.

Just like Dick Cheney in 2003 when the defense budget jumped from $280 billion to almost $400 billion, Lovett was not bothered by the vast defense expenditures projected by NSC 68: the U.S. economy "might benefit from the kind of build-up we are suggesting."[31]

What brings the Pentagon neoconservatives together with Burnham, Christopher Hitchens (another former Trotskyite), and some additional Trotskyites and Straussians I have known,[32] is their pretense of infallibility, their contempt for different opinions, an overweaning pride that imagines a lone, courageous individual taking on all comers, armored by ideological bona fides that they think give them an unassailable stance before the mere hoi polloi and an unfathomable egotism and self-regard. The only thing they share with Leo Strauss is the fantasy that ideas sway history (at times maybe they do, but not in America). Otherwise

they carry the signs of those most loathsome qualities of preten-
tious intellectual windbags: self-anointed omniscience and self-
proclaimed moral purity and absolutism.

Like Burnham, the Bush doctrine abjured deterrence and
valued liberation over containment. But it began with September 11, as if that watershed event founded the new strategy.
Those attacks did indeed come from an implacable and diabolical enemy: nothing will deter it, and it passionately loves suicide. Containment wouldn't scare Osama bin Laden, to say the
least, even if someone could find him. But little can be done
about that threat, the long-running "war on terrorism" not-
withstanding; it is still child's play to conjure up variations on
what calamity al-Qaida might think of next. The doctrine was
about a lover of homicide, Saddam Hussein, the other charter
members of the "axis of evil," and anyone else who might dare
to threaten American might and power—anywhere, anytime,
for eternity. And it is about fissures that go to the heart of the
Republican Party.

That party has long embraced two tendencies, the free-trade
multilateralism and Atlanticism of the eastern wing, and the ex-
pansionist, unilateralist western Republicans, symbolized by the
"Asia firsters" of the 1950s. The former was hegemonic on the
British model, taking the world economy as its main arena of
action; the latter was imperialist, beholden to the myths and realities of the frontier, the cowboy and the cavalry, unilateral
expansion to the West, the subjugation of the Philippines, and
eventually China (always, to these foreign affairs naïfs, the
"China" of their imagination). The reigning hero of this tendency
was Gen. Douglas MacArthur, a classic man on horseback, bru-
talizing the Bonus Marchers, suzerain of the Philippines, con-
queror of Japan thus to become its benign emperor for six years,
only to suffer defeat at the hands of a Sino-Korean peasant army
in 1950.

AN OBSCURE MATRIX OF DECISION

There is a curious, muffled fact about the post-1950 American role in the world that insiders understand, but that escapes the American public and most historians. It comes and goes in our media in the form of evanescent blips on the radar screen, momentary perturbations of the surface discourse that appear and disappear. The name of this Rumplestiltskin is precisely Burnham's "liberation" or "rollback." When Ronald Reagan invaded Grenada and knocked over a leftist regime, the State Department called it a "rollback." It might have been an island the size of Martha's Vineyard, but it was a triumph of liberation. Opponents of the way the first Bush war in the Middle East ended decried his failure in 1991 to "liberate" Iraq. Jake Garner, Bush Junior's first choice to head up the unilateral occupation of Iraq, a general who served two terms in Vietnam, told reporters that "We should have taken the war north instead of waiting in the south. Just like here [Iraq]. If President Bush had been president we would have won [in Vietnam]."[33] But mainstream policy makers and historians pretend that "liberation" was never more than a figment of John Foster Dulles's fervid imagination; the Burnhams of the world may rant, but they never rule.

For most of the postwar era Republican centrists like Dulles or Nelson Rockefeller or Henry Kissinger agreed with Cold War liberals in the Democratic Party on just about everything beyond the water's edge; there was a seamless consensus inside the Beltway on containment, internationalism, the NATO and U.S.-Japan alliances, and the iron necessity to consult with our allies at the UN or the IMF or the World Bank. Often the result was unilateralism disguised as multilateralism (Korea, Vietnam), but everyone bespoke the internationalist mantras and knew that the only lasting, sustainable hegemony is a consensual partnership, with the United States as first among (would-be) equals.

American combat troops first landed in Korea not in 1950, as we have seen, but on a pristine September day five years earlier. On another beautiful September day in 2001, the eleventh day, 37,000 of them were still in South Korea. Korea is the best example in modern history of how easy it is to get into a war, and how hard it is to get out. We barged into the thicket of Korean politics and culture, and have yet to find an exit strategy. But the stalwarts of the American national security consensus will say Korea was a just war that was carefully limited by Harry Truman, following the containment doctrine. Vietnam would have been the same, and indeed was essentially the same from the mid-1950s (when Washington committed its prestige to the Saigon government) to the mid-1970s when the war concluded with an American defeat—because the United States was unable to contain communism there, which in practice meant sustaining a stable Saigon regime and a permanently divided Vietnam. If we could have done so we would still be there, stuck in the aspic of another Korea. The Gulf War came to an end when Bush the Elder and his advisors, preeminently Brent Scowcroft, kicked on the brakes well short of Baghdad and thus spawned another containment system, leaving thousands of U.S. troops in bases in Saudi Arabia, the Gulf emirates, and elsewhere in the Middle East. Korea, like the Gulf War in 1990–91, fits in the national security lexicon under this title, a victory for containment.

The Korean War was the occasion for the quadrupling of defense spending in 1950 that built the American position at home and abroad, but another crisis could have stimulated the same thing, or provided the necessary funding for NSC 68, the central document of the Cold War that transformed containment into a global crusade. Approved by Truman in April 1950, it still lacked Congressional funding and support, and Truman was too weak a president to push it through in the absence of a major crisis.

"Korea came along and saved us," in Acheson's words in 1954, as Congress finally coughed up a huge peacetime defense budget in the midst of the Chinese intervention in late 1950. The Korean War's intrinsic importance to American history is, first, that it was the fulcrum for massive and permanent defense spending. Its greater importance to history, however, involved the provocative reversal of the containment doctrine into its opposite, "liberation," something never again repeated until Bush invaded Iraq.

War came in Korea after nearly a year of conflict within the Truman administration that had placed a new option on the agenda: liberation or "rollback" emerged as a genuine national security option in the course of interdepartmental deliberations leading up to NSC 48—the most important Asian policy document before the Korean War, signed by Truman at the end of December 1949. (It was this document that first approved military aid to the French in Indochina.) In August 1949 John Paton Davies wrote to Kennan that the United States could no longer afford "to follow indefinitely a policy of avoiding risks of conflict with [the Soviets] at whatever cost to us." He thought the initiative now rested in the "reckless hands" of the Communists, but that the United States could reverse that through the use of covert means, "coercion by punitive action," "coercion through a selective use of air power" (including limited air strikes on Manchuria), and the like. Of course, the United States "could not embark on such a course [intervention], even on a limited scale, until the Communists have so acted as to justify our retribution along the lines of this paper."[34] Later that month a State Department review committee produced the phrase that would later echo through NSC 48 and NSC 68, symbolizing the conjoining of containment and rollback. An unsigned paper on East Asia policy stated that the general objective of the United States should be to establish "free and independent governments," but "the objective of the immediate policy of the U.S. was to *check and roll back* in the [Asian] area the threat of Soviet Communism" (my emphasis). The Communists had seized the initiative, and the United States should get it back.

Another draft paper for NSC 48 written in October 1949 urged the government to recognize "the great advantages in cold war tactics of seizing and retaining the initiative through the prosecution of a coordinated [*six spaces still classified*] cold war offensive." A subsequent draft argued that Asia had "indigenous forces" which, "if effectively developed in aggressive pursuit of the cold war should be able by means short of war to *commence the rollback* of Soviet control and influence in the area" (my emphasis). This paragraph made its way into the final document, however, only after Acheson had made various revisions; like Colin Powell in the Bush administration, he was trying to control a president inexperienced in foreign affairs—and so he wanted "to emasculate NSC 48 before it caught the president's fancy."[35] The paper thus evolved to say that Asian indigenous forces could "assist the U.S. in *containing* Soviet control and influence in the area" (emphasis added). In other words, containment had to be added to an original draft thinking only of some sort of rollback. In the final versions of NSC 48 and NSC 68, the critical phrase became "to contain and where feasible to reduce" communist power in Asia. In other words, it collapsed the concern for rollback and for reducing the area of communist control into a realm of feasibility (where rollback might happen if it seemed likely to work), but reintroduced containment as the main point.

Many readers may think that these were mere contingency plans, that no one in the Truman administration really thought about offensive "positive action"; indeed, the idea that American planners, let alone officials like Davies (who later was run out of the State Department by Joe McCarthy), contemplated Asian rollback in the fall of 1949 would have been treated, at any point before the declassification of these documents, as the wildest rad-

ical claptrap. But the evidence is unimpeachable: this thinking
was new, serious, and a clear departure from previous assumptions, something manifest in internal critiques at the time. None
of the dissent was directed at the application of containment to
East Asia, which was the main purpose of NSC 48. But the new
emphasis on rollback drew immediate fire. S.C. Brown wrote in
October that NSC 48 reflected "an imposing collection of logical
absurdities." The "reduction" of Soviet influence, he said first off,
was "quite different from the concept of 'containment' of Soviet
power." This, he said, "is made perfectly clear by the reference to
a possibility of 'rolling back' communism." He said that the areas
cited for rollback included Manchuria and the Shanghai-Nanjing-
Beijing-Tianjin area (i.e., the major urban and industrial areas of
China, not mentioned in any document I found, and therefore
probably excised in the more central NSC documents by declassification censors), and then remarked, "this concept of 'reduction' goes far beyond anything I have ever seen used to describe
current U.S. policy toward the USSR, and clearly implies military
action of some sort."[36]

The Korean decision was, for Secretary of State Dean Acheson,
a defensive one to throw back the North Korean assault,[37] following on the containment logic he had elaborated three years
earlier when he told the Senate in secret session that the United
States had drawn the line in Korea. Within three weeks of the
invasion, however, key decision makers had turned the logic of
containment on its head, a sleight-of-hand not without some
black humor, in which the heretofore inviolable "international"
boundary at the 38th parallel, which when crossed by Koreans of
the northern persuasion had evoked Hitler-style aggression, was
now deemed permeable from the South. A low-level cold warrior
in the State Department, Everett Drumwright, wrote on July 10,
1950, that "once the rout starts it would be disastrous and stupid
of us to stop at the 38th parallel. . . . Our goal and the UN goal

is unification." (MacArthur commanded all forces under a "UN command" that was fictitious in practice—MacArthur sent press releases to the UN, rather than involve it seriously in his decisions—but that still exists, and was the spurious model recommended to the UN by the Bush administration for running post-invasion Iraq.) John Allison, somewhat higher on Foggy Bottom's greasy pole, was then stimulated to prepare a top-secret paper arguing that unlike the boundaries in central Europe the 38th parallel had no de jure significance (after all). The record, he said, showed "that this line was agreed upon only for the surrender of Japanese troops and that the U.S. had made no commitments with regard to the continuing validity of the line for any other purpose."[38] In other words the parallel bisecting Korea is an internationally recognized boundary if Koreans cross it, but not if Americans do.

John Foster Dulles, then an advisor to Truman, quickly gave Allison's paper to Dean Rusk, and the next day (July 14) Rusk penned a memo to Paul Nitze, arguing explicitly for a march into the North. When the Policy Planning Staff, still under George Kennan's influence, wrung its hands about the Kremlin possibly intervening against such an invasion, Allison wrote an "emphatic dissent." Soon Allison headed up the NSC study of rollback that resulted in the enabling document being tabled in September; NSC 81, embodying much of the language of Rusk, Allison, and Dulles was tabled in July. It was in Allison's top-secret paper of August 12, however, that the NSC 48/NSC 68 syllogism was patent: "Since a *basic policy* of the United States is to *check and reduce* the preponderant power of the USSR in Asia and elsewhere, then UN operations in Korea can set the stage for the noncommunist penetration into an area under Soviet control" (emphasis added). John Davies and others also wrote memoranda in August explicitly linking rollback in Korea to the "check and reduce" goals of previous policy.[39] The Defense Department also chimed in for

rollback: the course of the war had now provided "the first opportunity to displace part of the Soviet orbit," thus linking the
march north to the realm of feasibility pointed to in NSC 48.
This paper was unusually explicit in noting a side effect: that
Manchuria, "the pivot" of the Soviet Far East strategic complex
"would lose its captive status. . . . "[40]

President Truman approved the invasion of the North, according to the best evidence, at the end of August.[41] The decision
was embodied in NSC 81, written mostly by Rusk, which au-
thorized MacArthur to move into North Korea if there were no
Soviet or Chinese threats to intervene. It explicitly called for "a
roll-back"; the enabling order to MacArthur, sent on September 16,
referred to "the pursuance of a rollback." Truman's liberation of
the North was to be a "limited" one; he did not want the war
to expand into China. MacArthur, however, favored a rollback
in Korea as prelude to a rollback in China; if for him there was
"no substitute for victory," each victory called forth a new war.
Once the first troops crossed the parallel in early October, rollback was on everybody's lips. War dispatches routinely referred
to the "liberated areas" in the North. Charles Murphy remarked
that the United States should redouble its efforts "to look for
ways to wrest the initiative from the Soviets and to roll them
back." Oliver Edmund Clubb, also a subsequent victim of Mc-
Carthyism, wrote that "our problem is to begin to roll up the
satellites by positive action and not simply to remain in a defensive posture," and hoped that if the Chinese came into the war,
they would get a good bloodying. John Carter Vincent, another
of McCarthy's "Reds" in the State Department, weighed in from
his exile in Bern saying, "personally, I believe we should cross
the 38th parallel when set to do so irrespective of whether Chou
En-lai is bluffing or not."[42]

American troops rolled up to the Yalu River meeting little or
no resistance, mistaking a rapid withdrawal by North Korean

forces for a rout.[43] Meanwhile the air force sought to decapitate the North Korean leadership. (During the war on Iraq the world learned about the "MOAB" bomb, nicknamed the "Mother of All Bombs," weighing in at 21,500 pounds with an explosive force of 18,000 pounds of TNT. *Newsweek* put the bomb on its cover, under the title, "Why America Scares the World."[44] The war opened with cruise missiles raining down on a supposed meeting of Saddam and his top advisors.) In the desperate winter of 1950–51, Kim Il Sung and his closest allies were back where they started in the 1930s, holed up in deep bunkers in Kanggye near the Manchurian border. After failing to find them for three months after the Inch'ŏn landing (an intelligence failure that included a carpet-bombing campaign along the old Sino-Korean tributary route extending north from P'yŏngyang to the border, on the assumption that they would flee to China), B-29s dropped "Tarzon" bombs on Kanggye. This was an enormous new 12,000-pound bomb never before deployed,[45] but it failed to kill a single important North Korean leader. Nonetheless it was experiences like this, combined with American carpet-bombing of nearly everything standing and fifty years of American nuclear threats, that subsequently led the leadership to build underground national security structures to a degree perhaps unmatched in world history (there are as many as 15,000 below-ground installations in the North.)

After 200,000 Chinese intervened together with some 100,000 North Korean troops that P'yŏngyang had kept in reserve, they administered perhaps the worst defeat in American history before Vietnam: and finally everyone learned Kennan's lesson. Republicans like Dulles and Richard Nixon merged with Democrats like Dean Acheson on the central importance of containment: liberation or "rollback" had failed miserably, and had raised the specter of World War III; it couldn't be done against an ongoing communist system. Acheson later wrote that the decision to defend South Korea was the finest hour of the Truman presidency, but the decision to march to the Yalu occasioned "an incalculable defeat to U.S. foreign policy and destroyed the Truman administration." Here was "the worst defeat . . . since Bull Run." However Acheson assumed that the latter happened not to him but to his bête noire: Acheson successfully pinned the debacle in the North on MacArthur, and mainstream historiography has squared the circle in the same way.

The devastating impact of the defeat in northern Korea put decisive outer limits on rollback for the next several decades. Containment was the real Eisenhower policy, vastly preferable to the centrist elites then in control of foreign policy. John Foster Dulles, putative architect of liberation and rollback, was instrumental in placing these same limits: well before the 1956 Hungarian rebellion (usually thought to spell the end of his rollback fantasies), in secret meetings he castigated "preventive war" doctrines and liberation schemes: trying to detach satellites from the USSR, he said, "would involve the United States in general war." Later on Dulles searched for a place where a "mini-rollback" might be accomplished, its feasibility defined by getting in and out unscathed and not provoking the Chinese or the Russians. The paltry place of choice, which Dulles brought up frequently in NSC meetings in the 1950s, was Hainan Island off the Sino-Vietnamese coast. Like another rollbacker, Ronald Reagan at Grenada in 1983, Dulles was reduced to an "island" strategy, a quick-in, quick-out chimera. But of course Dulles never tried it.[46]

The Korean War thus fathered a virtual "stalemate machine" in Washington that governed one intervention after another, producing rapid entry but no effective exit. The boundaries on containment explain the bipartisan stalemate between conservatives and liberals over the Bay of Pigs in 1961, the unwillingness to invade the North during the Vietnam War, and the compromise on whether to contain or invade and destroy the Nicaraguan revolution throughout the 1980s (the ill-fated "Contras" along the Honduran border were the compromise result). Here was the Korean War–forged crucible that produced American anticommunist strategy, a containment doctrine that would work politically at home and strategically abroad and that explains the relative peace-and-quiet of the "North" during the Cold War. Out of this centrist unity came an unprecedented bipartisan commitment to containment and gigantic peacetime defense budgets, regardless of fiscal discipline, but no more serious attempts at "rollback." Perhaps the best symbol of this historical compromise is Eisenhower's defeat of Bob Taft at the Republican convention in 1952, which Burnham supported.

George Kennan understood that what we now call "American policy" in the 1940s and 1950s meant something much deeper— "*politics* on a world scale."[47] He became famously unhappy with the implementation of his containment doctrine, which expanded to a global crusade with NSC 68 and then turned into its opposite in Korea. But in 1994 he was also less sure of what the end of the Cold War meant than most analysts, and alluded briefly to the determining crisis in 1950–51:

> I viewed [containment] as primarily a diplomatic and political task, though not wholly without military implications. I considered that if and when we had succeeded in persuading the Soviet leadership that the continuation of the[ir] expansionist pressures . . . would be, in many respects, to their disadvantage, then the moment would have come for serious talks with them about the future of Europe. But when, some three years later [1950], this moment had arrived—when we had made our point with the Marshall Plan, with . . . the Berlin blockade and other measures—when the lesson I wanted to see us convey

to Moscow had been successfully conveyed, then it was one of the great disappointments of my life to discover that neither our Government nor our Western European allies had any interest in entering into such discussions at all. What they and the others wanted from Moscow, with respect to the future of Europe, was essentially "unconditional surrender." They were prepared to wait for it. And this was the beginning of the forty years of Cold War.[48]

If few Americans understand this critical turning point, neither do the usual suspects rounded up for foreign policy punditry on television. But the North Koreans know this episode in their bones, because it nearly extinguished their state. Therefore they will treat with absolute distrust and suspicion any president who comes along talking about "preemptive strikes," liberation, decapitation, and preventive war.

An uneasy coalition between the eastern and western wings of the Republican Party persisted into the 1960s, punctuated by the humiliation of Nelson Rockefeller at the Goldwater-dominated 1964 Republican convention, and Nixon choosing to move from California to New York City as the 1968 election campaign drew near. But since that time the stronger tendency has clearly been the West, bringing to the fore sunbelt Republicans like Ronald Reagan who were ostensible libertarians and fiscal conservatives, but who had no qualms about using military Keynesianism to lubricate the enormous government-corporate complex nourished by huge defense spending in the sunbelt states. (Dick Cheney and Don Rumsfeld, of course, are poster boys for how to work this military-industrial nexus to one's best career advantage, and how to create humongous deficits through Pentagon spending.) The most successful Republicans tried to ride both circuits, but there has really been just one master at this: Tricky Dick—a classic western Republican red-baiting "who lost China" unilateralist at one point in his career, an eastern internationalist at another, with his lasting triumph coming in the opening to Mao's China.

As a westerner, by the 1960s Richard Nixon understood the demographics of political realignment: air conditioning and massive water works made life livable for large populations in the vast humid or arid reaches of the sunbelt, and the 1964 Civil Rights Act had opened the entire South to any demagogue who wanted to use racist code words to separate the Democrats from their long-time base in the segregationist states. This "Southern strategy" brought into the Oval Office the darkest personality ever to inhabit it, and ushered in decades of Democratic ineffectiveness. But on foreign policy Nixon was a centrist, and always had been since he became vice president in 1952. He paid no attention to the Republican lunatic fringe, occupied for decades by people like H.L. Hunt or Billy James Hargis, railing on about a Rockefeller-Communist-UN conspiracy to found a socialist world government. After his first year, neither did Reagan.

Then suddenly the Cold War ended. Saddam invaded Kuwait. The Soviet Union collapsed. Sometimes history has a sense of humor; who could have imagined that George Herbert Walker Bush would preside over these momentous events—and would mainly be remembered for two metaphors: "a thousand points of light" (dimming quickly as the first Bush recession deepened) and "read my lips: no new taxes" (and along came new taxes). The Bush family history is a microcosm of ways to bring the eastern and western wings of the party together. The father is a thoroughly eastern Republican, born in Greenwich, combining internationalist foreign policy with great wealth and aristocratic privilege; his Texas credentials, honed since he moved there in the 1950s, never fooled anybody. His career in government was that of a charter member of the internationalist consensus and he was as persuasive at a tent revival as Dick Cheney at a labor rally.

George W. is not his father, he is the real thing, a Connecticut Yankee in H.L. Hunt's court who went Texan with a vengeance—and this became the horn of the dilemma in his administration. George the Second served as the feckless tabula rasa straddling two wings of the same party, like a cowboy on two horses. In domestic policy, he cultivated a conservative right wing that could not elect him (Bush the First was right about that), but he did so because of Karl Rove's dictum that Daddy failed them and thus lost the 1992 election. In foreign policy, however, his team of horses has run—always strenuously—in various and often opposite directions, stretching the logic of his diplomacy to the breaking point. As Bush bolted first in one direction and then another, his staggering around put our best friends on the permanent defensive, wondering what comes next, while doing little damage to our adversaries—and not nearly enough to the demonic al-Qaida. Usually the point of foreign affairs is to keep your allies happy and your enemies off balance: Bush invented a way to fire up and miss on all cylinders, while pushing our allies to their wits' end. And the internal divisions over North Korea were the worst, likened by Senator Joseph Biden to "the San Andreas fault."[49]

If the execution of foreign policy was Bush League, the Bush Doctrine was real and dangerous. In March 2003 the strategy of preemption quickly gave way to a preventive war against Saddam Hussein: he was fully contained in his "box," UN inspectors were all over the box, he wasn't about to attack anybody, but Bush invaded anyway because Saddam had "weapons of mass destruction" (yet to be found as of this writing). So far the war in Iraq has not had the worst consequences for regional security that many critics worried about, even if the occupation turned into

an unholy nightmare, but a restive world may present an una-
voidable crisis—most likely with North Korea—where containment and deterrence abruptly give way once again to preemption
and disaster.

George Kennan, a ninety-eight-year-old major leaguer, gave a
little-noticed interview to Albert Eisele just after the NSC released its new doctrine: here was "a great mistake in principle,"
Kennan said; anyone who has studied history "knows that you
might start a war with certain things in your mind," but you end
up fighting for things "never thought of before." Launching a
second war with Iraq "bears no relation to the first war against
terrorism," he thought, and anyway a decision for war "should
really rest with Congress." (But not with Congressional Democrats, who have been "shameful and shabby," not to mention
"timid," in their reaction to Bush's war plans.)

For more than a decade since the USSR disappeared Americans have watched the Pentagon and its many garrisons abroad
continue to soak up nearly one-third of the national budget, and
spend more than all our conceivable enemies combined; here is
a perpetual motion machine of ravenous appetite. An administration that began with talk about bringing troops home from
Clinton's ill-advised adventures and abjuring "nation building,"
soon asked taxpayers to underwrite "an aleatory expedition in the
management of the world's affairs," in the prescient words of
historian Charles Beard's original critique of containment.[50] Vital
interests are proclaimed where none existed before, temporary
expedients become institutional commitments, a thick web of
military and bureaucratic interest proliferates, the Pentagon bean
counters take over, every new appropriations season in Congress
becomes an occasion for defending this or that outpost (new or
old, vital or marginal)—and American power is mired in works
of its own doing.

Any administration would have responded forcefully to the

tragic attacks on September 11, but Bush and his allies have vastly expanded the Pentagon budget (from $265 billion in 2000 to $400 billion in 2003), added another zone of containment (Central Asia), created our own West Bank the size of California in Iraq, poured yet more billions into "Homeland Defense," and showed a callous disregard for civil liberties, the rights of the accused, and the views of our traditional allies. Many at the heart of the matter in the Pentagon resist this new crusade; Brig. Gen. Jared Kennish, who commanded troops in Kyrgystan, had this to say: "Here I am in a nation I had never heard of, couldn't pronounce and couldn't find on a map six months ago. . . . " Vice Admiral Lyle Bien told the same reporter, "We're developing a force that makes it almost too easy to intervene. I am concerned about America pounding herself out."[51] But the news media and Hollywood fawn on the American military and take jingoism to an embarrassing extreme. Major outlets like Fox News cater exclusively to an imagined audience from the "red" states of the 2000 election (or the 70 percent of the armed forces who voted for Bush). Patriotism is not simply the last refuge of scoundrels but the easiest thing in the world: it's harder, though, to hide the hypocrisy with which these shadow warriors feign to honor our dead soldiers in a parade of sentimentality and bathos.

In a classic article in 1941, Harold Lasswell defined "the Garrison State" as one in which "the specialists on violence are the most powerful group in society." North Korea is a classic garrison state, perhaps the best example in world history of a thoroughly militarized nation; this was their (unfortunate) answer to the defining crisis of the regime—occupation by an American army. But we are also well advanced toward a national security–dominated system, making the country of the founding fathers unrecognizable above all to them. The United States is hardly a country with a strong military tradition; you can count on the fingers of one hand the decades since 1789 when the U.S. military has been a powerful and respected factor in national life. Nor is the military the basic source of American power and influence in the world. There is a stronger countervailing tendency, hard to define but deeply influential in American history. The first thought that struck me after witnessing (on television) thousands of casualties resulting from an attack on the American mainland, for the first time since 1812, was that over the long haul the American people may exercise their longstanding tendency to withdraw from a world deemed recalcitrant to their ministering, and present Washington with a much different and eminently more difficult dilemma than the here-today, gone-tomorrow "axis of evil": how to rally the citizens for a long twilight struggle to maintain an ill-understood American hegemony in a vastly changed world.

THE GREATER EVIL: BUSH AND KIM JONG IL SINCE THE SUPREME COURT DECISION

It's too bad that Kim Jong Il can look so sinister when he wants to; his father presented such a smiling and handsome visage that sometimes it was impossible to imagine him shipping enemies off to the gulag or bureaucrats off to the mines. This prince perhaps has the face that life rather than nature has given him; like Bush he has to contend every day with the knowledge that he would not be where he is without Daddy's provenance. In any case that face is perfect for an American media that loves to front its stories and tales about the North with "Dr. Evil" affixed to the cover, thus doing Bush's work without being asked.[52] But what do we make of a magazine of record with a world-historical reputation for indefatigable fact-checking, namely the *New Yorker,* advertising a major article on the North under the caption, "How Crazy Is Kim?" and running a grainy photo of the Dear Leader (their translation of *chinaehanŭn chidoja,* a common phrase refer-

ring to beloved and benevolent leaders, i.e., the Confucian ideal)
sitting akilter behind huge dark glasses, with a look on his face
saying "This is not the time to take my picture"?[53] Our discourse
on foreign adversaries has become completely debased in a few
short years, even in the best outlets; we have a cartoon show
playing into the hands of a dangerous president, just as it denies
the American people the information and knowledge that would
allow them to become informed about the crises that this same
president seems to bump into with astonishing frequency. Osama
is crazy, Saddam is a beast, Arafat is a terrorist, Chirac is anti-
American, and Kim is Dr. Evil: would you say the media bats
.1000? I would say .200, one for five (Saddam was a beast), not
a good average.

When Santayana wrote about those who forget history he did
not mean the reductio ad absurdum today, in which many Americans or TV networks like Fox appear unaware that the only election George W. Bush won in 2000 was a 5-to-4 decision by the
Supreme Court in *Bush v. Gore*. Even less do they remember that
our never-ending problems with North Korea were on the verge
of a comprehensive solution at the same moment. In the month
before the presidential election the most powerful military man
in North Korea, Gen. Jo Myong Rok, who presides over the
military-industrial conglomerate that makes and sells DPRK missiles, visited Bill Clinton in the Oval Office and negotiated a
written pledge that "neither government would have hostile in-
tent toward the other." This was the essential prelude to Secretary
of State Madeleine Albright's unprecedented trip to North Korea
in late October to negotiate directly with Kim Jong Il, which was
in turn prelude to Clinton's impending summit in P'yŏngyang
(earlier Clinton had invited Kim to Washington, but Kim turned
him down), where the president would sign a deal to buy out all
of North Korea's intermediate and long-range missiles.

Who remembers that the good and substantial Madame deplaned in P'yŏngyang on October 23, 2000, wearing a heliotropic violet dress with matching floppy hat, bestirring a Russian friend to e-mail me and ask if this was not the most significant "hat" event since John Foster Dulles eyeballed Kim Il Sung across the 38th parallel a week before the invasion ("Foster up in a bunker with a Homburg on," Acheson later recalled; it was too funny for words). Or that she proclaimed the Dear Leader to be rational, if not quite normal? ("He is amazingly well-informed and extremely well-read," one American in the entourage said; "he is practical, thoughtful, listened very hard. He was making notes. He has a sense of humor. He's not the madman a lot of people portrayed him as").[54] Secretary Albright presented him with an NBA basketball signed by his basketball hero, Michael Jordan; Jong Il immediately wanted to take the ball out and dribble it around.

The missile agreement was the result of painstaking efforts by a State Department team led by former defense secretary William Perry, Under-Secretary Wendy Sherman, and mid-level officials who had patiently found ways to coax the North Koreans into various agreements over the preceding decade—all the while braving a hailstorm of right-wing Republican calumny, character assassination, and distorted and hysterical charges, most often voiced in the Moonies' *Washington Times*. As Perry put it, his team would seek "the complete and verifiable cessation of testing, production, and deployment of missiles exceeding the parameters of the Missile Technology Control Regime [MTCR], and the complete cessation of export sales of such missiles."[55]

Secretary of State Albright had this deal nailed down by November, except that the North agreed to give up only its medium- and long-range missiles, but would not agree to enter the MTCR unless President Clinton met Kim Jong Il in a summit in P'yŏngyang. Had the North entered the MTCR, all North Korean missiles above a range of 180 miles would have been eliminated, thus removing a threat felt deeply in nearby Japan. In return the United States would have provided some $1 billion in food aid to the regime, for an undetermined number of years.[56] In other words getting North Korea into the MTCR would cost $1 billion annually and a summit meeting between the American president and Kim Jong Il; National Missile Defense, for which North Korea was Don Rumsfeld's poster boy before September 11, had already cost the U.S. taxpayers $60 billion.

President Clinton wanted to go to P'yŏngyang, indeed his negotiators on Korea had their bags packed for weeks in November 2000—but as Clinton's national security advisor Sandy Berger later put it, it wasn't a good idea for the president to leave the country in November when they didn't know "whether there could be a major constitutional crisis."[57] After the Supreme Court stepped in to give the 2000 presidential election to George W. Bush, it was too late.

The new administration was quickly at loggerheads over whether there had been any real progress in Korea, or not. A day before President Kim Dae Jung showed up as the first foreign leader to meet with Bush in the White House in March 2001, Secretary of State Colin Powell told reporters that he would pick up where the Clinton administration left off in working toward a deal that would shut down North Korea's missiles. Soon he had to backtrack, caught short by the president's own hard line taken in his Oval Office meeting with Kim—a meeting that was a diplomatic disaster by any standard. Kim Dae Jung, fresh from winning the 2000 Nobel Peace Prize, was expecting to welcome the North Korean leader to Seoul in April or May of 2001, with this meeting being the follow-up to the unprecedented P'yŏngyang summit in June 2000. He returned home with his advisors publicly calling the meeting embarrassing and privately cursing President Bush.[58] Powell backed and filled and right-wing Republicans lambasted him for "appeasement," while President

Kim's upcoming summit and his "sunshine policy" were suddenly plunged into deep trouble, with P'yŏngyang abruptly canceling a cabinet-level meeting that had been scheduled in Seoul—and Kim Jong Il has yet to reciprocate by showing up in Seoul.

Months after Kim Dae Jung's visit, Bush appeared to reverse himself when the administration announced that it would be willing to talk with the North Koreans, after all. Newspapers reported that a policy paper from former ambassador to Korea Donald Gregg to former president Bush (Gregg was national security advisor to Bush when he was vice president) had wended its way to the Oval Office and turned the new president around on the issue. It was clear during the Clinton administration that an opening to North Korea had backing from nearly all centrist Democrats and Republicans, and Gregg was one of the vocal backers.

While Bush's advisors continued to argue over whether to confront or to engage P'yŏngyang, Kim Dae Jung's leading advisor on the North, Lim Dong Won, reopened high-level contacts in April 2002.[59] The North responded with energetic diplomatic activity for the next several months, renewing high-level talks with the South, making a number of agreements on re-linking railways and establishing new free-export zones in the North, continuing to marketize its own economy (if in fits and starts), culminating in Kim Jong Il's August meeting with President Putin and the unprecedented visit by Prime Minister Koizumi to P'yŏngyang in September 2002. In early 2003, however, Donald Gregg told an Ann Arbor audience that he was very pessimistic about a good outcome to the renewed crisis: the North had admitted to a second nuclear program, true, but Bush's world view was also a major problem. When he came into office he had no world view, Gregg said, an accurate understatement; but now his world view was informed entirely by "the Vulcan group," another name for the Rumsfeld-Cheney-

Wolfowitz-Perle-Bolton axis that brought us the invasion of
Iraq. And by then the White House didn't even bother to return
Republican Gregg's phone calls.

The second nuclear crisis with North Korea began in October
2003 with "sexed up" intelligence that was used politically to push
P'yŏngyang to the wall and make bilateral negotiations impossible. If our adversaries are caricatured in our media, the murky
business of "intelligence" is almost completely mystified. The
complacent American public seems unperturbed by Bush's failure
so far to find a single weapon of mass destruction in Iraq, but
the much more interested and disputatious British public was
immediately up in arms, so to speak, about the remarkable intelligence failures that preceded and were used to justify the
British-American invasion. To try and plumb the bottom of this
phenomenon one needs to be an indefatigable reader of our best
newspapers, in the venerable I.F. Stone mode. Take a long and
detailed article by Judith Miller, buried on page twelve of the
New York Times:[60] only in the thirtieth paragraph of this thirty-
four-paragraph article do we learn that prewar American intelligence on Iraqi "weapons of mass destruction" sites was often
"stunningly wrong," according to a senior U.S. officer:

> "The teams would be given a packet and a tentative
> grid," he said. "They would be told: 'Go to this place.
> You will find a McDonald's there. Look in the fridge.
> You will find french fries, cheeseburger [sic] and
> Cokes.' And they would go there, and not only was
> there no fridge and no McDonald's, there was never
> even a thought of ever putting a MacDonald's there.
> Day after day it was like that [in Iraq]."

This officer's "MET Alpha" group was sent to Basra to investigate
"highly suspicious equipment" identified by the "Iraq Survey

Group" in U.S. intelligence, which might well be components for nuclear weapons. The team found "a handful of large, industrial-scale vegetable steamers," their crates clearly and accurately marked as such in Russian.

Bush White House reporter David Sanger of the *New York Times* made his career with so many "scoops" from U.S. intelligence that some of his colleagues just call him "Scoop." Unfortunately not a few have been wrong. A decade ago he was capable of turning a public CIA statement that North Korea *might* have one or two atomic bombs into an accepted fact, in the space of one article. In August 1998 the *Times* front-paged his story that U.S. intelligence had found a huge underground facility where North Korea was secretly making nuclear weapons; when the North allowed the U.S. military to inspect this site a few months later they found it empty, with no traces of radioactive material ever having been there.[61] On July 19, 2003 the *Times* led the news with a Sanger article (co-written with Thom Shanker) again claiming that U.S. intelligence had found "a second, secret plant for producing weapons-grade plutonium." A senior Bush administration official told the *Times* that this information was "very worrisome, but still not conclusive." The evidence consisted of "elevated levels of krypton 85," a gas given off when nuclear fuel is converted to plutonium, in regions quite removed from the Yŏngbyŏn complex where the North maintains its only declared reprocessing facility. South Korean experts immediately denied this story, and David Albright, one of the best and most reliable experts on nuclear weapons technology, said it was inherently impossible to pinpoint a hidden or secret location merely from detecting elevated levels of krypton 85. Meanwhile the North can do uranium (as opposed to plutonium) enrichment at many spots in the country, in small enough amounts that krypton 85 emissions would not rise above their normal environmental level.[62]

The payoff in the Sanger/Shanker article was again on the inner pages in the last paragraphs, where the problem became *not* a second plutonium facility, but the inherent difficulties if Bush were to mount a preemptive strike on the North's nuclear installations, given their recent dispersal to "any number of other locations." The *Times* also, for the first time in my daily reading, said that the North had as many as 15,000 "underground military-industrial sites," and a history of "constructing duplicate facilities" such that it may well have "multiple facilities for every critical aspect of its national security infrastructure."[63] Such facts have been known to experts for some time, but they pose a bit of a problem for preemptive strikes, as we will see, leading the Bush administration to plan instead for a series of massive attacks against the North, using nuclear weapons.

Where did the CIA mantra about "one or two bombs" come from? It was first included in a National Intelligence Estimate in November 1993, an estimate arrived at by gathering all the government experts on North Korea together and asking for a show of hands as to how many thought the North had made atomic bombs. A bit over half raised their hands. Those in the slim majority assumed that the North Koreans had reprocessed all of the fuel they removed prior to 1994 (about 11 kilograms), and that they had done the arduous work of fashioning an implosion device. After this vote the CIA director annually told Congress that "the chances are better than 50/50" that the North had one or two bombs. Yet three years later nuclear experts at the Livermore and Hanford labs reduced their estimate of how much fuel the North had to less than the amount needed for a single bomb; they thought the North could only have seven or eight kilograms of fuel, yet "it takes ten kilograms of weapons-grade plutonium to fabricate a first bomb," and eight or nine kilograms for subsequent ones. David Albright also concluded independently that "the most credible worst-case estimate" is that the North may have 6.3 to 8.5 kilograms of reprocessed plutonium.[64] The CIA's

50/50 educated guess appears to be mistaken, in other words. Less obvious was its role in strengthening the North's position in negotiations with the United States.

It was left to the Bush administration and its emissary James Kelly, however, to vastly exaggerate the North's atomic prowess by claiming to have unearthed a second nuclear program to enrich uranium, and then confronting the North with that "intelligence" during face-to-face meetings in P'yŏngyang held a few short weeks after Bush published his preventive war doctrine. But Bush delayed the release of this damning information until he got his Iraq war–enabling resolution through Congress; as one U.S. official put it, "the timing of this [North Korean] thing is terrible."[65]

The North predictably responded by saying *yes*—we have that and a lot more too! (But the subsequent Bush policy of ignoring its own evidence that the North now had two bomb programs and refusing to call it a "crisis" befuddled North Koreans. As one DPRK general told a Russian visitor, "When we stated we don't have a nuclear weapon, the USA [said] we do have it, and now when we are [saying] we created nuclear weapons, the USA [says] we're just bluffing."[66]) In other words *both* governments, in the words of a knowledgeable specialist who spent most of his career at the RAND Corporation, "opted to exploit the intelligence for political purposes." And thus began the unraveling "of close to a decade of painfully crafted diplomatic arrangements designed to prevent full-scale nuclear weapons development on the Korean Peninsula. By year's end both countries had walked away from their respective commitments under the U.S.-DPRK Agreed Framework of October 1994."[67]

RAND veteran Jonathan Pollack is not the sort of analyst who usually departs from Beltway judgments, but he argued that Bush's intelligence estimates "offered more definitive claims" about the North's nuclear capabilities than previous intelligence reports had, and seemed to fudge the date when the CIA discovered all this. It was 1997 or 1998, and the Clinton administration had fully briefed the incoming Bush people in 2000–01 on this program, yet Kelly and others left the impression that the program had just been uncovered in the summer of 2002. Kelly never presented "specific or detailed evidence to substantiate" his claims, either in P'yŏngyang or to the press when he returned home, nor did he ask his DPRK interlocutors for explanation or clarification of whatever evidence he may have brought with him. Within days the administration told the *New York Times* that the Agreed Framework was dead,[68] and shortly thereafter it cut off the heavy heating oil Washington had been providing as interim compensation under the 1994 agreement. In quick response P'yŏngyang declared that the 1994 agreement had collapsed and proceeded to withdraw from the Nuclear Non-Proliferation Treaty, kick out UN inspectors, remove their seals and closed-circuit cameras from the Yŏngbyŏn complex, regain control of 8,000 fuel rods that had been encased for eight years, and restart their reactor. (Basically this was a lock-step recapitulation in a few short weeks of what they had done in 1993–94 to get Clinton's attention.)

The American press immediately accepted Kelly's judgment that the North Koreans were big cheats who had failed to honor their agreements, and the nuclear enrichment program took on a life of its own in our mimetic media—repeated endlessly to tar and degrade North Korea. In November 2002, however, the CIA reported that a gas centrifuge facility for enriching uranium was "at least three years from becoming operational" in the DPRK; once up and running it might provide fissile material for "two or more weapons per year." But in March 2003 Kelly told Congress that the facility (assuming there is one; U.S. intelligence can't find it) is probably "a matter of months" away from producing weapons-grade uranium.[69] Left unmentioned in any press articles that I came across, was the extraordinary utility of an enriched uranium program for the light-water reactors (LWRs) that were being built to compensate the North for freezing their graphite reactors in 1994. The virtue of the LWRs from the American standpoint was that their fuel would have to come from outside the DPRK, thus establishing a dependency relationship that could easily be monitored; but this was the vice of the LWRs for the independent-minded North. As Pollack put it, "it seems entirely plausible that P'yŏngyang envisioned the need for an indigenous enrichment capability . . . the fuel requirements for a pair of thousand-megawatt [light-water] reactors are substantial and open-ended."[70] Furthermore uranium enrichment to a level useful for LWR fuel is much easier than the further refinement necessary to create fissile fuel. But the Bush administration smothered all discussion of this issue with widely ballyhooed claims of a second nuclear bomb program.

Many knowledgeable experts, including former Clinton administration officials, believe that North Korea clearly cheated on its commitments by importing these technologies. They do not accept the argument that the North had a clear interest in enriching uranium for the LWRs. Assuming that the imports of this technology from Pakistan began in 1997 or 1998 and were intended for use in a bomb, it may have happened because hardliners disliked the slow pace by which Washington was implementing its commitments from the 1994 agreement (i.e., to normalize relations with the North and refrain from threatening it with nuclear weapons), or Kim Jong Il may have chosen to play a double game, honoring the Framework Agreement while developing a clandestine weapons program. He ascended to maximum power in September 1998 on the fiftieth anniversary of the founding of the regime, and may have sought to shore up his support in the military with a new program. These same former U.S. officials, however, believe that whatever the North planned to do with its nuclear enrichment technology could have been shut down in the context of completing the missile deal and normalizing U.S.-DPRK relations. That was essentially what they told the incoming administration in 2001. By dropping the ball on this matter and dithering for eighteen months, only to use the information to confront the North Koreans in October 2003, the Bush people turned a soluble problem into a major crisis, leaving little room to back away on either side.

The acute danger in Korea, though, really derives from a combination of typical and predictable North Korean cheating and provocation, longstanding U.S. war plans to use nuclear weapons in the earliest stages of a new Korean War, and Bush's new preemptive doctrine. This doctrine conflates existing plans for nuclear preemption in a crisis initiated by the North, which have been standard operating procedure for the U.S. military for decades, with the apparent determination to attack states like North Korea simply because they have or would like to have nuclear weapons like those that the United States still amasses by the thousands. As if to make this crystal clear, someone in the White House leaked presidential decision directive 17 in September 2002, which listed North Korea as a target for preemption.

Pentagon closet warrior Donald Rumsfeld made matters even worse in the spring of 2003 by demanding revisions in the basic war plan for Korea ("Operations Plan 5030"). Unnamed senior Bush administration officials considered elements of this new plan "so aggressive that they could provoke a war." The basic strategy, according to insiders who have read the plan, is "to topple Kim's regime by destabilizing its military forces," so they would overthrow him and accomplish a "regime change." The plan was pushed "by many of the same administration hard-liners who advocated regime change in Iraq." Short of trying to force a military coup, Rumsfeld and company want the U.S. military to "stage a weeks-long surprise military exercise, designed to force

North Koreans to head for bunkers and deplete valuable stores of food, water, and other resources."[71]

This is how the 1950 invasion began: North Korea announced a long summer military exercise along the 38th parallel, mobilizing some 40,000 troops. Once the war games started, several divisions suddenly veered south and took Seoul in three days; only a tiny handful of the highest officials knew that the summer exercises were prelude to a blitzkrieg. Larry Niksch, a longtime specialist on Asian affairs at the Congressional Research Service and a person never given to leaps toward unfounded conclusions, cited Rumsfeld's new war plan and wrote that "regime change in North Korea is indeed the Bush administration's policy objective." If recent, sporadically applied sanctions against the DPRK and interdiction of its shipping do not produce a regime change or "diplomatic capitulation," then Rumsfeld planned to escalate from a preemptive strike against Yŏngbyŏn (which Clinton came close to mounting in 1994) to "a broader plan of massive strikes against multiple targets."

The United States terrorized North Korea with nuclear weapons during and after the Korean War and was the only power to introduce nuclear weapons to Korean soil. Beginning in 1958 it deployed hundreds of nuclear warheads, atomic mines, and artillery shells, and air-dropped nukes in South Korea. They remained until 1991, when Bush the Elder withdrew battlefield nuclear weapons from around the world—which of course did not end the nuclear threat to the North, since Trident submarines (sometimes called a holocaust in one delivery package) can glide silently up to its coast any day of the week.[72] In the aftermath of the initial nuclear deployments Kim Il Sung openly said that the North's only recourse was to build as widely and as deeply underground as possible, on the assumption that anything visible above ground would be wiped clean in a war. I have seen one such nuclear blast shelter, at the bottom of a very steep escalator in a P'yŏngyang subway station where three gigantic blast doors, each about two feet thick, are recessed into the wall. Hans Blix was astonished when he conducted the first UN inspections of the Yŏngbyŏn nuclear site in 1992 to find "two cavernous underground shelters," access to which required "several minutes to descend by escalator." They were built, Blix was told, in case someone attacked the complex with nuclear weapons.[73] United States commanders in the South have said in recent years that they believe nearly the entire military apparatus of this garrison state is now ensconced underground.

Half a century later comes Mr. Rumsfeld, who according to two eyewitnesses was surprised to learn when he joined the Pentagon that we still had nearly 40,000 troops in Korea. The vehicles for his "massive strikes" are newly developed missiles that penetrate deeply underground before detonating a "small" nuclear explosive. In 2003 he sought a Congressional repeal of the decade-old ban on manufacturing small nuclear weapons. "[Congressional] proponents, mainly Republicans, argue[d] that low-yield [nuclear] warheads could be used to incinerate chemical or biological weapons installations without scattering deadly agents into the atmosphere." But the Bush administration thought "low-yield" nukes would be more effective in deterring "emerging nuclear powers like North Korea and Iran." These new earth-penetrating weapons would have hardened casings (probably made of depleted uranium) enabling them "to crash through thick rock and concrete."[74]

The Spratt-Furse Amendment of 1993 prohibited research and development of low-yield weapons, defined as having "the explosive force of less than five kilotons of TNT," approximately one-third the size of the Hiroshima bomb that incinerated 100,000 people and radiated another 80,000 to death. Senate opponents argued that repealing this bill would signal the death-knell of efforts at non-proliferation: "We're driving recklessly down the road that we're telling other people not to walk down," said Michigan senator Carl Levin.[75] Because of opposition from Levin, Diane Feinstein (D-CA), and others, the bill had not passed the Senate as of this writing.

The only problem with Rumsfeld's war plan is that it repeals the laws of physics: there is no technology yet developed or imagined that can penetrate the earth's surface more than about fifty feet. This is why cruise missiles could not decapitate Saddam Hussein on the night the Iraq invasion began, assuming he was in the building; later inspections revealed deep and heavily reinforced chambers designed by a German firm to withstand a direct hit with nuclear weapons. So the only answer is larger and larger nuclear warheads, such that you target Kim Jong Il and wipe out a large urban neighborhood, or maybe a city.[76]

Before the occupation of Iraq dimmed their clairvoyant powers on matters of war and peace, Rumsfeld, Wolfowitz & Company imagined that Kim Jong Il was running around like an ant on a frying pan in dread of decapitation. Kim disappeared from public view for fifty days in mid-February. Once he surfaced again, "a senior Defense Department official" (most likely Rumsfeld or Wolfowitz) told the *New York Times*, "Truly, if I'm Kim Jong Il, I wake up tomorrow morning and I'm thinking, 'Have the Americans arrayed themselves on the peninsula now, post-Iraq, the way they arrayed themselves in [pre-]Iraq?'" The United States wanted to get its own forces in Korea out of the range of the North's artillery guns, the official said, and then increase reconnaissance and newly configured deployments thus to "use precision targeting much more aggressively and much more quickly." In pursuit of this, during the buildup immediately preceding the invasion of Iraq the Pentagon moved twenty-four long-range B-1 and B-52 bombers from bases in the United States to Guam, and installed several F-117 stealth fighter-bombers in our bases in South Korea—"designed for quick strikes against targets ringed by heavy air defenses."[77] (The F-117s, of course, were the strike force that sought to decapitate Saddam on the day the Iraq invasion began.) Soon Wolfowitz was in Seoul to announce a redeployment of U.S. combat forces south of the Han River to get them out of harm's way, and in passing to opine to the world press that "North Korea is teetering on the brink of collapse."

"Post-Iraq" was May 12—the Vulcan Group crowing and contemptuous of any opinion different from its own. The United States remains a belligerent in the war that never ended, just as does North Korea. These provocative actions in the spring of 2003 might well have instigated another Korean War, given what had just happened in Iraq; short of that, they shame this nation in their ineffable combination of arrogance and ignorance.[78] Loud in prattling about American sovereignty when it comes to the United Nations, these officials see no other country whose sovereignty they are bound to respect. Furthermore they don't know what they are talking about. Kim Jong Il's birthday is February 16, a national holiday, and long disappearances (particularly during the harsh winter) have been a trademark of his rule. Here he husbands his "quality time," puttering around one of his villas in pajamas and curlers, trying to tame his unruly hair.[79] A better indication of the North's attitude is their statement on April 18 that "the Iraqi war teaches a lesson that in order to prevent a war and defend the security of a country and the sovereignty of a nation it is necessary to have a powerful physical deterrent force" (the euphemism they have used since James Kelly's October 2002 visit to suggest that they might have nuclear weapons).[80]

The best guess about Kim's response to such provocation might be this: in recent months North Korea has said many times that it would not wait around while the United States marshals the necessary resources to mount an attack against it, as Saddam did in the six months leading up to the Iraq war. They will do what "Little Bill" did in the classic film *Unforgiven*: after beating "English Bob" to a pulp and railroading him out of town, Little Bill shouted after him that if he ever laid eyes on the man again he wouldn't ask questions: he would just come out firing. Clearly the North Koreans do not want war; even amid these dire American threats, they used the same clipped April 18 news release to signal for the first time that they were willing to meet the United States in multilateral talks: "if the U.S. has a willingness to make a bold switchover in its Korea policy, we will not stick to any particular dialogue format." But it would be a foolish mistake to assume that if war comes to them, they won't go down fighting.

MULTILATERAL MACHINATIONS

After James Kelly's visit Bush adopted a strategy of refusing to talk to the North about anything except how it would go about dismantling its nuclear program—and refused bilateral talks even for this purpose. It offered no incentives in return, thus achieving the petrified immobilism that arises when one party is asked to give up everything and the other party, nothing—including its preventive war doctrine. The requirement that any talks be multilateral, however, was aimed primarily at East Asian allies whom Bush perceived to be getting off the reservation. Since the Nixon era, Republicans have had an affinity for the dictators who ruled South Korea for three decades. Nixon looked the other way in 1972 when Park Chung Hee declared martial law and made himself president for life; Reagan invited Chun Doo Hwan to the Oval Office shortly after the inauguration as his first visiting head of state, after Chun had trampled over the population of Kwangju, killing hundreds if not thousands, on the way to making his 1980 coup; many Korean election specialists remain convinced that a Republican team jiggered the vote-counting computers during the 1987 presidential election that brought

Chun's protégé, Roh Tae Woo, to power. In 2002 the Bush administration seemed to think the candidate of the old ruling party, Lee Hoi Chang, had a lock on the next presidential election. Instead the Korean people elected Roh Moo Hyon, a courageous lawyer who defended many dissidents against the Chun and Roh Tae Woo regimes. Roh Moo Hyon had campaigned on a platform of establishing more independence and equality in the Korean-American relationship, and of continuing his predecessor Kim Dae Jung's policy of reconciliation with the North.

After Roh Moo Hyon's election the American press was full of rhetoric about "anti-Americanism" in the South, and scare stories about Korean ingrates wanting to kick U.S. forces out of the country. "There are already signs of a deep distrust of Mr. Roh in the Bush administration," a reporter wrote just before Roh's inauguration; a senior U.S. military analyst opined, "Kim Jong Il would probably attack our troops on the DMZ and then pick up the phone to Roh and say . . . 'You must do something to stop the Americans.' " A "regional security expert" at Nanzan University in Japan, Robyn Lim, declared that "the U.S. alliance with South Korea is defunct."[81] Around this time advisors to Roh told Bush administration officials that if the United States attacked the North over South Korean objections, it would destroy the alliance with the South. Another anti-American comment? Imagine how you would feel if a distant power wanted to make war on Canada without consulting Washington, while Canada targeted our population with an impregnable phalanx of 10,000 embedded artillery guns.

Roh's victory was the first democratic election involving two major candidates in which the winner got close to a majority since 1971, when Park Chung Hee barely eked out a victory over Kim Dae Jung's 46 percent of the vote, in spite of all sorts of regime manipulation (Park then decided there would be no more elections). But it occasioned a remarkable petulance, coming even (or perhaps especially?) from Americans who have long experience in Korea. Richard Allen, a Republican point man on Korean affairs who was often registered as an agent of the ROK by the U.S. Justice Department,[82] wrote in the *New York Times* that Roh Moo Hyun's election made for "a troubling shift" in U.S. relations with the ROK. Allen thought Korean leaders had now "stepped into the neutral zone" and had even gone so far as to suggest, in the current nuclear standoff, that Washington and P'yŏngyang should *both* make concessions: "the cynicism of this act constitutes a serious breach of faith." Maybe American troops should be withdrawn, Allen suggested, "now that the harm can come from two directions—North Korea and violent South Korean protesters." In Allen's opinion the United States "is responsible for much of Seoul's present security and prosperity," the implication being that Koreans shouldn't bite the hand that feeds them.[83]

Other Americans wondered how Koreans would dare criticize the United States, when North Korea is "rattling a nuclear sword"? A Pentagon official explained, "It's like teaching a child to ride a bike. We've been running alongside South Korea, holding on to its handlebars for fifty years. At some point you have to let go."[84] Another U.S. military official in Seoul said of Roh's election, "There is a real sense of mourning here [on his military base]."[85] Meanwhile American business interests stated that troop withdrawals would cause investors to "seriously reconsider . . . their plans here."[86] This remarkable combination of petulant irritability and grating condescension somehow seems unremarkable both to the people who say such things, and sometimes to the reporters who quote them.

A recent Korea Gallup Poll showed an increase in Koreans who "disliked the United States" from 15 percent in 1994 to 53 percent in 2003. News reports on this poll did not give the actual questions posed to respondents, but when asked the opposite question—do you like the United States?—the response was 64 percent in 1994, 37 percent in 2003.[87] Putting these results another way, 36 percent of people surveyed in 1994 said they disliked the United States—not a particularly comforting figure. More to the point, there is little to indicate one way or the other whether such poll results stem primarily from the Bush administration's policies and the U.S. military's acquittal of two U.S. soldiers who ran over and killed two teenage girls, or from a growing "anti-Americanism." But one 2002 poll for the *Sisa Journal* found that 62 percent of the Korean respondents thought that Bush's policies toward North Korea had not been helpful.[88]

Meanwhile Japanese prime minster Koizumi was planning his own breakthrough to the North. Over many months, negotiations for a summit between Koizumi and Kim Jong Il "had been conducted with the utmost secrecy" within the Japanese government. After a secret visit to P'yŏngyang in August 2002, an advisor to Koizumi said the North Koreans were receptive to anything he might want to discuss, including allegations that the North had kidnapped Japanese citizens in the past. On August 27, 2002, Koizumi finally decided to tell the Bush administration about his plans, when Deputy Secretary of State Richard Armitage was visiting Tokyo. This P'yŏngyang summit made huge news when it was announced on August 30. As Jonathan Pollack wrote, "the absence of prior communication between Japan and the United States on the prime minister's impending visit was remarkable enough in its own right. In the context of recent intelligence findings about North Korea's [nuclear] enrichment activities, the prime minister's last-minute disclosure . . . was even more stunning to American officials."[89]

Soon James Kelly was in Tokyo, where he spent three days tabling his evidence about the North's nuclear enrichment program and trying to dissuade Koizumi from his determination to meet Kim Jong Il in P'yŏngyang. He failed, Koizumi took off in mid-September, and Kim Jong Il took the unprecedented step of admitting that his regime had kidnapped Japanese, for espionage purposes (most likely for identity theft, but also perhaps to create agents in Japan). The summit and the major agreements concluded there disappeared quickly in the maelstrom of Japanese outrage, beamed to the nation 24/7 by television. Instead of a diplomatic breakthrough, Koizumi had a huge public relations problem on his hands. A few weeks later Mr. Kelly showed up in P'yŏngyang to confront the North with this same "evidence" (never disclosed to the American public), which had the effect of derailing a further rapprochement between P'yŏngyang and Tokyo, and later provided a club to pressure the Roh Moo Hyun administration back into the fold of a multilateral, unified front against North Korea.

I happened to be in Seoul when Koizumi's summit was announced, a day or two after John R. Bolton (carrying the euphemistic title of "under secretary of state for arms control" in an administration that has wrecked arms control) arrived to denounce Kim Jong Il personally and his regime more generally as evil, a menace to peace, the greatest security threat in the region, and the like. He did so again in the summer of 2003, as six-party talks on the North Korean problem were about to be held in Beijing. A brutal tyrant had North Korea in the grip of "a hellish nightmare," he said among other things, causing Richard Armitage publicly to distance himself from Bolton's hot rhetoric.[90] Bolton was a Barry Goldwater right-winger in his youth and later a protégé of Senator Jesse Helms (who over many decades showed his warm regard for the various anticommmunist tyrants that the United States supported around the world, especially those in Central America). When a reporter from the *New York Times* asked Bolton what the Bush policy was toward the North, "he strode over to a bookshelf, pulled off a volume and slapped it on the table. It was called *The End of North Korea,* by an Amer-

ican Enterprise Institute colleague. 'That,' he said, 'is our policy.' "[91]

It is the president's policy, too. From the beginning of his
term Bush has denounced Kim Jong Il as an untrustworthy madman, a "pygmy,"[92] an "evildoer," and in a recent discussion with
Bob Woodward, he blurted out "I loathe Kim Jong Il!," shouting
and "waving his finger in the air." In a less noticed part of this
outburst, Bush declared his preference for "toppling" the North
Korean regime.[93] (One gets the sense from these impromptu *ad
hominem* eruptions that Bush's resentments might have something to do with the widespread perception that both leaders owe
their prominence to Daddy.) John Bolton is a favorite of the
president's, and ventriloquist[94] Dick Cheney is said to be the
hardest of hard-liners on the North. But this man who slid into
office after the closest election in American history may be the
most belligerent of all.

Shortly before the fiftieth anniversary of the Korean War ar-
mistice, former defense secretary William J. Perry gave a harrow-
ing interview to the *Washington Post*. He had just finished
extensive consultations with senior Bush administration officials,
South Korean president Roh Moo Hyun, and senior officials in
China. "I think we are losing control" of the situation; he said,
we are on a "path to war." North Korea might soon have enough
nuclear warheads to begin exploding them in tests or exporting
them to terrorists. "The nuclear program now underway in
North Korea poses an imminent danger of nuclear weapons being detonated in American cities," he charged—an absurdity, in
my view, since in retaliation we would turn the North into "a
charcoal briquette" (Colin Powell's expression). Perhaps Perry
was trying to get Bush's attention, or highlight his hard-line bona
fides for the Beltway crowd. But then Perry got to the main
point: he had concluded that Bush just won't enter into serious
talks with P'yŏngyang: "My theory is the reason we don't have

a policy on this, and we aren't negotiating, is the president himself. I think he has come to the conclusion that Kim Jong Il is evil and loathsome and it is immoral to negotiate with him."[95] Thus do an insecure, reclusive dictator and an insecure, impulsive foreign affairs naïf hold the peace of the world in their hands—according to a former official who knows as much about our Korea policy as anyone. A less alarmist and hopefully more accurate view came from a fine young scholar who knows as much about Korean security as anyone: "The fundamental difference between Clinton's near-success and Bush's stalemate [with the North] lies . . . in his refusal to end the enmity between the two nations."[96]

BACK TO THE FUTURE?

Secretary of State Powell gained control—perhaps temporarily—of Korea policy during the heat of the Iraq war (causing the Vulcan Group to complain that they were too distracted to block what he was doing[97]) and convinced Bush to allow James Kelly to meet the North Koreans again, in Beijing in April 2003, and then to participate in six-party talks that China moved heaven and earth to arrange at the end of August. David Sanger heralded the result of the talks as a sign that the Bush administration had fundamentally altered its approach toward the North, at the urging of the State Department. The mess in Iraq had enhanced Secretary Powell's stature, another reporter wrote, and Bush had decided he needed help from our UN allies and friends after all (but "the question is whether the world is ready to pick [them] up off the floor and dust them off. A lot of people aren't ready yet," said a Western diplomat).[98] Time will tell if Bush's sudden desire for talks with the North and assistance from other countries really signifies a change; optimistic analysts said similar things when Powell took the Iraq problem to the United Nations in September 2002. If so, and Bush gets an agreement, he will only return matters to the achievements of the Clinton administration that were offered to him on a silver platter in 2001.

For more than a decade the North Koreans have been trying to get American officials to understand that genuine give-and-take negotiations on their nuclear program can be successful around the terms of a "package deal" that they first tabled in November 1993. Instead of the Bush policy of all-or-nothing-at-all, the North has steadfastly said it would give up its nukes and its missiles in return for a formal end to the Korean War, a termination of mutual hostility, lifting of numerous economic and technological embargoes that the United States maintains on the North, diplomatic recognition, and direct or indirect compensation for giving up these very expensive programs. Their will to do so was tested in 1994, when they froze their entire nuclear complex and kept it frozen under the eyes of UN inspectors for eight years, until Bush made it crystal clear that he would not fulfill the American side of the 1994 bargain. Two authors recently revived a "grand diplomatic bargain" to accomplish about the same thing, an ambitious and complex program that is worth a careful perusal by anyone concerned with the issues: in return for a verifiable end to the North's nuclear programs, a ban on selling and testing its missiles, a steep cut in its conventional forces, outward-opening economic reforms, and the beginnings of a dialogue about human rights in the North (or the lack thereof), Washington should be ready to respond with a non-aggression pledge, a peace treaty that would finally end the Korean War, full diplomatic relations, and an aid program of "perhaps $2 billion a year for a decade" (that burden to be shared with our allies). They muster a host of nuanced, clever, and convincing arguments on behalf of their strategy, with the ultimate goal being "a gradual, soft, 'velvet' form of regime change—even if Kim Jong Il holds onto power throughout the process."[99] We will have that, or we will have more dangerous drift in U.S. policy, or we will have a terrible war. Unfortunately for the time being this choice is not in the hands of the people, but a capricious administration that listens to nobody, and a jumpy group in P'yŏngyang.

Having said all this, there are still many Americans who may or may not like George Bush, but who will think that the North Korean regime is among the most despicable on earth (I watched a former U.S. ambassador to Japan lecture President Roh Moo Hyun on this point at a Blue House meeting on the day after Roh's inauguration), and for a tyrant like Kim Jong Il to get his hands on nuclear weapons would be a calamity to be stopped at all costs. I would urge those Americans to remember that 23 million human beings live in the North, that the leadership has had huge piles of chemical weapons for decades, and perhaps biological weapons; we deterred them from using such weapons for half a century with our nukes, and if they deter the warmongers among the Pentagon civilian appointees with those same weapons, that is a predictable and perhaps even a stabilizing outcome. In any case there is nothing we can do about it, short of a catastrophic war that will destroy Northeast Asia, cause untold needless deaths, and demolish the Bush administration. Furthermore it does not dignify the United States to have an enemy like this; rather it demeans this great country. And the unthinking, uninformed, bigoted, but seamlessly uniform pillorying of the North in our media is a symptom of a deeper disturbance. The "North Korean problem" is an outgrowth of a truly terrible history going all the way back to the collapse of the world system in the Great Depression, a history through which the Korean people have suffered beyond measure and beyond any American's imagination. We could have solved the North Korean problem decades ago but our leaders have chosen not to try (with the exception of Bill Clinton), and in this new century we are all the worse for it.

RECOMMENDED READING

Armstrong, Charles K. *The North Korean Revolution, 1945–1950.* Ithaca and London: Cornell University Press, 2003.

Cumings, Bruce. *The Origins of the Korean War*, 2 vols., Princeton: Princeton University Press, 1981, 1990; Seoul: Yoksa Pip'yong-sa, 2003.

Cumings, Bruce. *War and Television: Korea, Vietnam and the Gulf War.* London: Verso; New York: Visal-Routledge, 1993.

Grinker, Roy Andrew. *Korea and Its Futures: Unification and the Unfinished War.* New York: St. Martin's Press, 1998.

Han Hong-koo. *Wounded Nationalism: The Minsaengdan Incident and Kim Il Sung in Eastern Manchuria.* Seattle: University of Washington Press, forthcoming.

Harrison, Selig S. *Korean Endgame: A Strategy for Reunification and U.S. Disengagement.* Princeton: Princeton University Press, 2002.

Ienaga, Saburo. *The Pacific War, 1931–1945*, trans. Frank Baldwin. New York: Pantheon Books, 1975.

Lankov, Andrei. *From Stalin to Kim Il Sung: The Formation of North Korea, 1945–1960.* London: Hurst & Company, 2002.

Lee, Chong-sik. *Counter-Insurgency in Manchuria: The Japanese Experience, 1931–1940.* Santa Monica: The RAND Corporation, 1967.

O'Hanlon, Michael and Mike Mochizuki. *Crisis on the Korean Peninsula: How to Deal with a Nuclear North Korea.* Washington, D.C.: McGraw-Hill (A Brookings Institution Book), 2003.

Oberdorfer, Don. *The Two Koreas: A Contemporary History*. New
    York: Addison-Wesley, 1997.

Park, Han S., ed. *North Korea: Ideology, Politics, Economy*. Engle-
    wood Cliffs, N.J.: Prentice-Hall, 1996.

Rosegrant, Susan, in collaboration with Michael D. Watkins.
    "Carrots, Sticks, and Question Marks: Negotiating the
    North Korean Nuclear Crisis." Harvard University, John F.
    Kennedy School of Government, 1995.

Sigal, Leon V. *Disarming Strangers: Nuclear Diplomacy with North
    Korea*. Princeton: Princeton University Press, 1998.

Suh, Dae-sook. *Kim Il Sung: The North Korean Leader*. New
    York: Columbia University Press, 1988.

Wada, Haruki. *Kim Il Sŏng kwa Manju Hang-Il Chŏjaeng* [Kim
    Il Sung and the anti-Japanese War in Manchuria]. Trans.
    from the Japanese by Yi Chong-sŏ. Seoul: Ch'angbi-sa,
    1992; published also in Japanese as *Kin Nichi-sei to Manshu
    konichi senso*. Tokyo: Heibonsha, 1992. (Unfortunately as
    yet there is no translation into English.)

NOTES

1. Quoted from *The Gulag Archipelago* by David R. Loy, "The Non-Duality of Good and Evil: Buddhist Reflections on the New Holy War," *Pacific Rim Report*, no. 25 (October 2002), 1.
2. See Cumings, *North Korea: Another Country* (New York: The New Press, 2003), chap. 3. We now have definitive histories of Kim's guerrilla struggle and his rise to power. See the books in the "Recommended Reading" list by Andrei Lankov, Haruki Wada, Charles Armstrong, Dae-sook Suh, and Han Hong-koo.
3. See Cumings, *The Origins of the Korean War*, vols. 1 and 2.
4. American intelligence worried mightily from 1943 onward that Korean guerrillas in Manchuria, whom the State Department associated with either Soviet or Chinese communism, would come to power in postwar Korea.
5. Leslie Gelb, "The Next Renegade State," op-ed page, *New York Times*, April 10, 1991.
6. From the 1979 English translation of Ienaga's classic, *The Pacific War*.
7. Gordon Prange, *At Dawn We Slept: The Untold Story of Pearl Harbor* (New York: Penguin Books, 1981), 539.
8. Charles E. Neu, "1906–1913," in Ernest R. May and James C. Thomson Jr., eds., *American–East Asian Relations: A Survey* (Cambridge: Harvard University Press, 1972), 155–72.

9. Quoted in Charles Beard, *President Roosevelt and the Coming of the War, 1941: A Study in Appearances and Realities* (New Haven: Yale University Press, 1948), 244–45, 418, 519, 526–27. See also Richard N. Current, "How Stimson Meant to 'Maneuver' the Japanese," *Mississippi Valley Historical Review* 40, no. 1 (1953), 67–74.

10. Bill Moyers, "Which America Will We Be Now?," *The Nation*, November 19, 2001, 11–14.

11. Widely reported on July 2, 2003.

12. Cumings, *The Origins of the Korean War*, vol. 1, 125–27.

13. Leon V. Sigal, *Disarming Strangers: Nuclear Diplomacy with North Korea* (Princeton: Princeton University Press, 1998), 184; Selig S. Harrison, *Korean Endgame: A Strategy for Reunification and U.S. Disengagement* (Princeton: Princeton University Press, 2002), 184.

14. Benninghoff to the State Department, September 15, 1945, in *Foreign Relations of the United States*, hereafter *FRUS*, 6 (1945), 1049–53.

15. Kim and some sixty guerrillas in his band tried to return to Korea through Sinŭiju on the Chinese border, but bombing had destroyed the bridges and so they left from Vladivostok on the Russian ship *Pugachev*, disembarking at Wŏnsan on September 19. Although a Soviet transport deposited these men in Korea, they returned independently of Soviet authorities (Wada, *Kim Il Sŏng kwa Manju Hang-Il Chŏnjaeng*, 341–43). See also Andrei Lankov's account, using formerly secret Soviet documents to show that Kim was not the hand-picked favorite of the Russians, who saw him as a military rather than a political figure.

16. *FRUS* 6 (1945), 1122–24.

17. Ibid., 1129–33.

18. Cumings, *The Origins of the Korean War*, vol. 2, 205.

19. *FRUS* 6 (1945), 1144–48.
20. *FRUS* 8 (1946), 706–709.
21. Roy Andrew Grinker, *Korea and Its Futures: Unification and the Unfinished War* (New York: St. Martin's Press, 1998), 271.
22. Excerpts from Memorandum of Conversation with USSR Ambassador to the DPRK, Comrade V.P. Moskovsky, concerning the negotiations between a Soviet delegation, led by Chairman of the USSR Council of Ministers Kosygin, and the KWP leadership, which took place on the 13th and 16th of February 1965 at the USSR embassy in the DPRK. Archive of the Central Committee of the Czechoslovak Communist Party, Collection 02/1, File 96, Archival Unit 101, Information 13, 1962–66, translated by Kathryn Weathersby and e-mailed to me by a friend.
23. All quotations from the "The National Security Strategy of the United States," September 20, 2002, as paginated when printed off the *New York Times* website (in their "printer-friendly" mode), 5, 11, 23.
24. Ibid., 12.
25. The *New York Times* on September 20, 2002, quoted this phrase from "a senior administration official," but David Sanger later attributed these remarks directly to Dr. Rice. See Sanger, *New York Times*, September 28, 2002, A17.
26. To my knowledge Bush first used the term "rid the world of evil" three days after the 9/11 attacks. See Loy, "The Non-Duality of Good and Evil," 2.
27. James Burnham, *The Struggle for the World* (New York: John Day Co., 1947), 4–14, 48–55, 134–64, 181–83, 203, 228–36, 239; John P. Diggins, *Up from Communism: Conservative Odysseys in American Intellectual History* (New York: Harper & Row, 1975), 163–64, 322.
28. Burnham's involvement with the Office of Policy Coordina-

tion, the covert action arm of the CIA at the time, is well documented. See for example Daniel Kelly, *James Burnham and the Struggle for the World* (Wilmington, Del.: ISI Books, 2002), 149–51. This new biography celebrates Burnham as "the first neo-conservative" who was right about all our encounters with communism—that is, he thought the USSR, China, North Korea, North Vietnam, and Cuba should have all been "rolled back," even if it meant preemptively attacking and obliterating them with nuclear weapons. Kelly gives us a Burnham stripped from his times and viewed through the dark glass of contemporary right-wing political correctness; perhaps a more formidable mind will one day write a better biography.

29. Townsend Hoopes, *The Devil and John Foster Dulles* (Boston: Little, Brown & Co., 1973), 118; also *FRUS* 1 (1950), 140–41, McFall to Webb, January 26, 1950.

30. R.A. Wormser to A.A. Berle, Dana C. Backus, Joseph L. Broderick, and Donovan, February 20, 1950, William Donovan Papers, box 76B. The committee is not identified, but seems to be a subcommittee of the New York Bar Association. All those named were prominent Wall Street lawyers.

31. *FRUS* 1 (1950), 196–200, "Meeting of State-Defense Policy Review Group," March 16, 1950. Lovett had gone back to Wall Street, identified here merely as a "banker."

32. Burnham the one-time Trotskyite was later labeled the "first neo-conservative," leading some commentators to connect a strange set of dots between contemporary political passions, the collapse of western communism, the civilian neo-cons who advise Bush, the philosopher Leo Strauss, and the University of Chicago. (See for example Michiko Kakutani, "How Books Have Shaped U.S. Policy," *New York Times*, April 5, 2003, D7. Leo Strauss's daughter subsequently

wrote a letter to the *Times* decrying this absurd association.)

Teaching at the University of Chicago always offers un-expected surprises, but this one I would never have predicted. It is true that the political science department (mis-)educated Wolfowitz and Perle when they were young men, mainly it would appear through the venue of Albert Wohlstetter. It is also true that Leo Strauss taught there for much of his career, and Straussians are still mainstays of the place. But so far as I know, Strauss was an intellectual of extraordinary depth and seriousness, a man of striking humility in spite of his talents, and a teacher whom students would be lucky to hear once in a lifetime. It is really Allan Bloom, Frances Fuku-yama, Saul Bellow, and others who have tried to connect these dots, above all Bellow in his nonfictional novel *Ravel-stein*, which depicts Bloom calling up Wolfowitz at odd hours to offer his opinions on U.S. foreign policy. The hard-nosed Straussians at Chicago dismissed Bloom as a popularizer, and Fukuyama's understanding of Nietzsche and Hegel in *The End of History* is so sophomoric as to embarrass the univer-sity. (See Cumings, "Time of Illusion: Post–Cold War Vi-sions of the World," in *Cold War Triumphalism*, ed. Ellen Schrecker [New York: The New Press, 2004].)

A brilliant little book by Laurence Lampert places Nietz-sche squarely at the center of Strauss's attentions throughout his adult life, matched only by Plato; Strauss correctly saw Nietzsche as the preeminent philosopher of the modern, but Strauss couldn't stand modernity and therefore shrunk from accepting Nietzsche's formidable teaching into an intellec-tual life lived vicariously in fifth-century Athens—a perfectly conventional thing for a cloistered professor to do. But Lampert notes that Strauss was honest enough to know when he had met his match. See Laurence Lampert, *Leo*

Strauss and Nietzsche (Chicago: The University of Chicago Press, 1996), 3, 30–59.

33. Quoted in the *New York Times*, April 15, 2003, B8.
34. National Archives, State Department PPS files, Davies to Kennan, August 24, 1949, box 13.
35. Michael Schaller, *The American Occupation of Japan: The Origins of The Cold War* (New York: Oxford University Press, 1985), 206.
36. National Archives, State Department Office of Chinese Affairs, box 15, S.C. Brown to Philip Sprouse, October 24, 1949, formerly top secret.
37. On July 12 Acheson said the United States had to fight back up to the parallel, no matter what. If it were pushed off the peninsula, it would have to "come back in." But the United States should not widen the fighting to China. After reoccupying southern Korea, the United States would have to garrison it and support it in the future: "as the Virginians say, we have bought a colt." But the colt was named containment. (Truman Library, Acheson Papers, box 65, Acheson memo for "Paul," July 12, 1950).
38. National Archives, State Department 795.00 file, box 4265, Drumwright to Allison, July 10, 1950; Allison, "The Origin and Significance of the 38th Parallel in Korea," July 13, 1950. Although this memo is unsigned, Dulles's memo to Rusk the same day refers to "Allison's memorandum with reference to the 38th parallel."
39. *FRUS* 7 (1950): Allison draft memo of August 12, 1950, 567–73.
40. *FRUS* 7 (1950): Dulles to Nitze, July 14, 1950, 386–87; PPS draft memo, July 22, 449–54; Allison to Nitze, July 24, 458–61; Defense Department draft memo, July 31, 1950, 502–10. See also 795.00 file, box 4266, "Future US Policy with respect to North Korea," July 22, 1950.
41. Rosemary Foot, *The Wrong War: American Policy and the*

Dimensions of the Korean Conflict, 1950–1953 (Ithaca: Cornell University Press, 1985), 74.

42. On "liberated areas," see many documents in National Archives, 795.00 file, box 5696; Murphy quoted in Truman Library, PSF, NSC file, box 220, 68th NSC meeting, October 2, 1950; Clubb quoted in 611.93 file, box 2860, Clubb to Rusk, October 26, 1950; *FRUS* 7 (1950): Vincent to State, October 7, 1950, 902; Clubb to Rusk, November 4, 1950, 1038–41.

43. See Cumings, *The Origins of the Korean War*, vol. 2, chap. 21.

44. Cover story, "Why America Scares the World," *Newsweek*, March 24, 2003.

45. Truman Library, PSF, CIA file, box 248, report of December 15, 1950; FO317, piece no. 84074 and no. 84075, Bouchier situation reports, December 5 and December 17, 1950; *New York Times*, December 13, 1950, January 3, 1951.

46. See my extended discussion in *The Origins of the Korean War*, vol. 2, chap. 22.

47. Kennan's italics, in Robert Latham, *The Liberal Moment: Modernity, Security, and the Making of Postwar International Order* (New York: Columbia University Press, 1997), 147.

48. *New York Times*, March 14, 1994, op-ed page. Kennan added, "Those of my opponents of that day who have survived [read Paul Nitze] would say, I am sure, 'You see. We were right. The collapse of the Soviet Union amounted to the unconditional surrender we envisaged. . . . And we paid nothing for it.' To which I should have to reply: 'But we did pay a great deal for it. We paid with forty years of enormous and otherwise unnecessary military expenditure.' "

49. Biden quoted in *USA Today*, April 25–26, 2003.

50. Beard, *Roosevelt and the Coming of the War*, 592–93, 597.

51. Greg Jaffe, "Pentagon Prepares to Scatter Soldiers in Remote Corners," *Wall Street Journal*, May 27, 2003, A1, A6. However the deputy commander of the Manas Air Field near Kry-

gyz, Col. James Forrest, told Jaffe that "this place is so deep into Central Asia you'd hate to lose it," a good indication that this former Soviet base is not likely to be "lost" to the Pentagon.

52. The cover story of the January 13, 2003, issue of *Newsweek* carried a photo of Kim Jong Il, "North Korea's Dr. Evil." On the cover of *Newsweek*'s first issue after the death of Kim Il Sung in July 1994 was this racist title: "North Korea: The Headless Beast."

53. *The New Yorker*, September 8, 2003, 54–66. The long article by Philip Gourevitch was better than most in American magazines, but it had a number of erroneous facts and judgments in spite of *New Yorker* fact-checking. *The Economist* featured Kim Jong Il looking contemptuous of something or somebody on its May 3–9, 2003, cover with a long-range missile arcing into the sky behind him.

54. Doug Struck and Steven Mufson, "North Korea's Kim Sheds Image of 'Madman,'" *Washington Post*, October 26, 2001, A1.

55. This is from the public version of Perry's report to the president, submitted in mid-October 1999.

56. See Michael R. Gordon's investigative report, "How Politics Sank Accord on Missiles with North Korea," *New York Times*, March 6, 2001, A1, A8. It so happened that I had lunch with William Perry a few days after this article appeared, and he confirmed it in every detail.

57. Quoted in Gordon, *New York Times*, March 6, 2001, A8.

58. An unnamed advisor said it was "embarrassing" in the *Korea Herald*, March 13, 2001; I spoke with a Korean member of the National Assembly at a conference on Korea on March 13, who talked about Kim's advisors cursing Bush for his ham-handed tactics.

59. Subsequently Lim said he had taken a "very long and detailed

letter" from President Kim to DPRK leader Kim Jong Il. In the letter, President Kim emphasized that since the September 11 attacks "the global strategy of the United States has fundamentally changed," and that the United States "is prepared to resort to military means of counterproliferation," so Kim Jong Il must "clearly understand that North Korea itself is also included in the possible targets." Reuters News Service, Martin Nesirky quoting a speech by Lim Dong Won in Cheju City, April 12, 2002.

60. Judith Miller, "A Chronicle of Confusion in the U.S. Hunt for Hussein's Chemical and Germ Weapons," *New York Times*, July 20, 2003, A12.

61. I discuss these Sanger articles in *North Korea: Another Country*.

62. Albright cited in Glenn Kessler, "Proposals to North Korea Weighed," *Washington Post*, July 22, 2003, A1.

63. Thom Shanker with David Sanger, "North Korea Hides New Nuclear Site, Evidence Suggests," *New York Times*, July 20, 2003, A1, A6.

64. Sigal, *Disarming Strangers*, 95; Harrison, *Korean Endgame*, 263. Albright thought 8.5 kilograms might be "just enough" for a single bomb.

65. "Bush's Strategy Is Complicated by North Korea," *Wall Street Journal*, October 18, 2002, A1.

66. Dr. Alexander V. Vorontsoz visited the DPRK recently, and I am grateful to him for sending me a copy of his recollections of the visit.

67. Jonathan D. Pollack, "The United States, North Korea, and the End of the Agreed Framework," *Naval War College Review* (Summer 2003), 1, 13. (I read this on the Internet and so my pagination may not follow the published article.) Dr. Pollack is now teaching at the Naval War College.

68. David E. Sanger, "U.S. to Withdraw from Arms Accord

with North Korea," *New York Times*, October 20, 2002, A1.

69. David E. Sanger, "U.S. Sees Quick Start of North Korea Nuclear Site," *New York Times*, March 1, 2003, A1.

70. Pollack, "The United States, North Korea, and the End of the Agreed Framework," 15.

71. Bruce B. Auster and Kevin Whitelaw, "Pentagon Plan 5030, A New Blueprint for Facing Down North Korea," *U.S. News and World Report*, July 21, 2003.

72. See my detailed discussion in *North Korea: Another Country*.

73. "Nuclear Site in North Korea Provides Clues on Weapons," *New York Times*, May 17, 1992.

74. James C. Dao, "Senate Panel Votes to Lift Ban on Small Nuclear Arms," *New York Times*, May 10, 2003, A2.

75. Ibid.

76. I am indebted for this information to several discussions with Stephen Schwartz, the editor of the *Bulletin of the Atomic Scientists*. He also presented a paper to this effect at a symposium in Japan on August 1, 2003, held to commemorate the fifty-eighth anniversary of the obliteration of Hiroshima. (I also spoke at this symposium.)

77. Thom Shanker, "Lessons from Iraq Include How to Scare Korean Leader," *New York Times*, May 12, 2003, A9. Rumsfeld's provocations came in spite of Secretary Powell's attempt "to assure the North Koreans that we are not looking to overthrow them, to take them out." See David E. Sanger, "Bush Takes No-Budge Stand in Talks with North Korea," *New York Times*, April 17, 2003, A11.

78. Perhaps the most memorable couplet in Graham Greene's *The Quiet American*. Rumsfeld also dreamed up a laughable scheme to team up with China and oust the North Korean regime—and told it to the press just a few days before U.S. negotiators met in Beijing with the North Koreans, a meeting arranged through great effort by China. See Sanger, "Admin-

istration Divided Over North Korea," *New York Times*, April 21, 2003, A15. The only conclusion appears to be that Rumsfeld tried mightily to sabotage any possibility of solving our problems with North Korea through give-and-take diplomacy.

79. See Cumings, "The World's First Postmodern Dictator," chap. 5 in *North Korea: Another Country*.

80. Korean Central News Agency (P'yŏngyang), April 18, 2003.

81. All quotes from Howard W. French, "U.S. Approach on North Korea Is Straining Alliances in Asia," *New York Times*, February 24, 2003, A9.

82. See Cumings, "The Korea Lobby," Japan Policy Research Institute, 1996.

83. Richard V. Allen, "Seoul's Choice: The U.S. or the North," *New York Times*, January 16, 2003, op-ed page.

84. James Dao, "Why Keep U.S. Troops?" *New York Times*, January 5, 2003, Week in Review, 5.

85. Howard W. French, "Bush and New Korean Leader to Take Up Thorny Diplomatic Issues," *New York Times*, December 21, 2003, A5.

86. Tami Overby, an employee of the American Chamber of Commerce in Seoul, as quoted in James Brooke, "G.I.s in South Korea Encounter Increased Hostility," *New York Times*, January 8, 2003, A10.

87. "Anti-U.S. Sentiment Deepens in South Korea," *The Washington Post*, January 9, 2003, A1, A18.

88. Howard W. French with Don Kirk, "American Policies and Presence Are Under Fire in South Korea, Straining an Alliance," *New York Times*, December 8, 2002, A10.

89. Pollack, "The United States, North Korea, and the End of the Agreed Framework," 17.

90. Christopher Marquis, "Absent from the Korea Talks: Bush's Hard-Liner," *New York Times*, September 2, 2003, A3.

91. Ibid.

92. If Kim Il Sung was tall, handsome, and charismatic, standing over six feet with a broad forehead prized by Korean mothers and aestheticians, the son looked just like his mother—a formidable woman, nurturing, kind and fun-loving, but less than five feet tall, standing pear-shaped in her guerrilla uniform. But where her face is round, wide, smiling, endearing, optimistic, six decades later his is round, wide, frowning, off-putting, and cynical. And he sees himself as a pygmy: ergo the unkind cut from the forty-fifth president. During her sojourn in the North, a South Korean movie actress found that Kim didn't like his body—he wasn't "comfortable in his own skin," to use the current cliché. Indeed, he thought he looked like "a little turd."

93. Bob Woodward, *Bush at War* (New York: Simon & Schuster, 2002), 340. In typically convoluted syntax, Bush referred to what would happen "if we try to—if this guy were to topple." Some people thought the "financial burdens" of such an outcome would be too onerous, but not the president: "I just don't buy that. Either you believe in freedom, and want to—and worry about the human condition, or you don't."

94. William F. Buckley was once asked if he coveted a position in the White House, and he immediately shot back, "Yes: ventriloquist."

95. Thomas E. Ricks and Glenn Kessler, "U.S., N. Korea Drifting Toward War, Perry Warns," *Washington Post*, July 15, 2003, A14.

96. Jae-Jung Suh, "The Two-Wars Doctrine and the Regional Arms Race," *Critical Asian Studies* 35, no. 1 (2003), 21.

97. "There's a sense in the Pentagon," one intelligence official said, "that Powell got this arranged while everyone was distracted with Iraq. And now there is a race over who will control the next steps." Sanger, "Administration Divided Over North Korea," *New York Times*, April 21, 2003, A15.

98. David E. Sanger, "U.S. Said to Shift Approach in Talks with North Korea," *New York Times*, September 5, 2003, A1; see also Steven R. Weisman, "Bush Foreign Policy and Harsh Reality," ibid., A1, A9.

99. Michael O'Hanlon and Mike Mochizuki, *Crisis on the Korean Peninsula: How to Deal with a Nuclear North Korea* (Washington, D.C.: McGraw-Hill/A Brookings Institution Book, 2003), 19, 50. For another road map toward peace in Korea, see "Turning Point in Korea," the report of the Task Force on U.S. Korea Policy, Sponsored by the Center for East Asian Studies, University of Chicago, and the Center for International Policy, Washington, D.C., 2003. (I co-organized this task force with Selig S. Harrison.)

2

EMPIRE STRIKES BACK:
IRAN IN U.S. SIGHTS

Ervand Abrahamian

Every ten years or so, the United States needs to pick up
some crappy little country and throw it against the wall, just
to show the world that we mean business.

—Michael Ledeen of the American Enterprise Institute

The question people are asking is why do they hate us? This
is the wrong question. . . . The question which we should
be asking is why they neither fear nor respect us.

—Professor Bernard Lewis

Oderint dum metuant (let them hate so long as they fear).

—Emperor Caligula

INTRODUCTION

The United States is on a collision course with Iran. The main
casualty could well be the democratic movement in Iran. Ever
since the Islamic Revolution of 1979, two separate themes have
shaped the U.S. media coverage of Iran. The first has been the
prospects of improved relations between the two countries. The
revolution had metamorphosized Iran from a close ally policing
the Persian Gulf for the United States into an intractable foe
threatening to export revolution throughout the Middle East.
The 1997 election of President Muhammad Khatami, a liberal
cleric who had campaigned to replace the "clash" with the "dialogue of civilizations," raised hopes for a détente. These hopes,

however, were dashed in 2002 when President Bush named Iran together with Iraq and North Korea as his "axis of evil." He also accused Iran of harboring secret programs to develop nuclear weapons. By 2002–2003, the nuclear issue had moved to the forefront of U.S.-Iran relations. The second theme has been the ongoing struggle between reformers and conservatives within the Islamic Republic. The reformers strive to extend the republic's democratic features; the conservatives are determined to preserve its theocratic features. By 2002-2003, the reformers, campaigning on the theme of curtailing clerical power, were winning landslide victories in presidential, parliamentary, and local elections. It seemed only a matter of time before they would force the conservatives to make major constitutional concessions.

The "axis of evil" speech threatens to reverse the process. Although billed as supporting "Iranian citizens who risked intimidation and death on behalf of liberty, human rights, and democracy," the speech has had the exact opposite consequences. It has created a mood of the "country in imminent danger," conjuring up ghosts of the past, especially of the 1953 coup and of two centuries of Western imperialism. It has emboldened conservatives with the argument that all patriots should rally together, that the notion of "dialogue" is naïve, and that "homeland security" is the most vital issue of the day. It has persuaded some reformers to tone down their public demands; others to put their hopes on the back burner waiting for better days. It has also energized exiles—especially Pahlavi royalists—who dread reform and hope that ultraconservative obstinacy will bring about a revolution. Those who have no hope of coming to power through reform hope to achieve it through a revolution—but a revolution launched by the United States.

U.S. POLICY

For the average Iranian, the "axis of evil" speech came as a bolt out of the blue sky. Relations between Iran and America had gradually but markedly improved in the course of the previous five years. In 1998, soon after his election, President Khatemi held out an olive branch by appearing on CNN and stressing the need for "dialogue among civilizations."[1] He praised the "great American civilization" built on Plymouth Rock and the ideals of the Puritan Pilgrims. He also implied that the hostage crisis had been "excessive," "a pity," and an unfortunate "tragedy." The Clinton administration reciprocated. It stopped labeling Iran as a "rogue" and "pariah" state." It described the 1953 coup as a "setback" for Iran, and for the first time admitted that the United States had "orchestrated the overthrow of Iran's popular prime minister, Mohammad Mossadeq."[2] It relaxed the draconian economic sanctions imposed since 1979: Iranian pistachios, caviar, and rugs were again permitted into the United States; and American wheat, medicines, and spare airplane parts were allowed to be exported to Iran. Moreover, former senior policy makers, such as Zbigniew Brzezinski, Brent Scowcroft, and Richard Murphy, spoke out in favor of ending "dual containment"—a policy that had been imposed against Iran as well as Iraq.

When September 11 struck, Iran wasted no time in holding the "terrorist Taliban" responsible and permitted ordinary citizens to hold night street vigils to express sympathy for America. Jack Straw, the British foreign minister, rushed to Tehran for what he termed a "historic visit." He thanked Iran for its help over Afghanistan and declared that "Iran stood together with Britain in opposing terrorism of any kind."[3] Colin Powell, the U.S. secretary of state, shook hands with the Iranian foreign minister, and told the press that Tehran would be included in the coalition against terrorism. In return, Iranian leaders announced that they were willing to resume normal diplomatic relations with the United States—relations that had been cut ever since the hostage crisis of 1979. When the United States invaded Afghanistan, Iran offered to rescue stranded pilots, opened up its ports for the transit of humanitarian aid, and urged the anti-Taliban Northern Alliance whom it had armed to fully cooperate with the Americans. What is more, Iran was instrumental in Geneva in brokering a deal by which Hamid Karzai, the American favorite, was nominated as president of Afghanistan. A Khatami confidant told reporters that "Afghanistan provided the two countries a perfect opportunity for improved relations."[4] American diplomats admitted in Congress that Iranians had been "extremely helpful in getting Karzai in as the president. They had even walked arm-in-arm with American negotiators in Geneva."[5]

The axis speech—together with the follow-up State of the Union Address—were multiple bombshells. They lumped Iran together with Iraq and North Korea as dangerous states pursuing weapons of mass destruction. They described Iran as "repressed by an unelected few" and as a "major exporter" of terrorism. They depicted the Afghan campaign as "only just the start of the war against terror"—clearly implying that countries like Iran would soon be targeted. They even spoke of preemptive strikes against future possible threats. "The United States of America," declared President Bush, "will not permit the world's most dangerous regimes to threaten us with the world's most destructive weapons."[6] Of course, the rhetoric and potency of the message was compounded by loaded terms derived from Christianity and World War II.

The speech sounded especially ominous coming soon after the unveiling of the Bush doctrine in a document entitled *National Security Strategy of the United States of America*. This doctrine openly advocated preemptive military strikes against countries deemed to be potential dangers to the United States. For the first time in history, the United States favored preemptive wars and thus contradicted international law as well as it own previous policies. As Brian Urquhart noted, this is a truly radical doctrine "striking at the heart of three fundamental texts that should be guidelines for foreign policy": the Treaty of Westphalia, the UN Charter, and the Nuremberg Court.[7] Similarly, Arthur Schlesinger noted: "During the long years of the cold war, preventive war was unmentionable. Its advocates were regarded as loonies."[8]

It was not only Iranians who were taken aback by the axis speech. It was soon leaked that Colin Powell and the State Department had not been consulted about the speech—neither about its general thrust nor about the inclusion of Iran.[9] Officials from the State Department complained privately that the Pentagon had hijacked foreign policy and that the speech would undermine their long-standing policy of rapprochement with Iranian reformers.[10] Powell's deputy remarked that some neoconservatives were in dire need of psychotherapy. A former member of the National Security Council commented that the axis speech signified the Pentagon's "triumph" over the State Department.[11]

Although the axis speech took many unawares, it was not a surprise for those familiar with neoconservative influence in Washington—especially in such think-tanks as the Project for the New American Century, American Enterprise Institute, Washington Institute for Near East Policy, Foreign Policy Institute, Center for Security Policy, and the Jewish Institute for National Security Affairs. These neoconservatives, known among more conventional conservatives as neo-rightists and neo-crazies, have persistently complained for years about Washington's "dovish" and "appeasement" policies towards "fascists" and "Islamic fanatics." They have also advocated redrawing the map, undoing Sykes-Picot (the Anglo-French division of the region during World War I), disregarding the Oslo Accords, and spreading democracy with "regime changes" throughout the Middle East.

Neoconservative influence in the Bush administration cannot be underestimated. As Donald Rumsfeld stated in a message to the Center for Security Policy, "If there is any doubt about the power of your ideas, one has only to look at the number of Center associates who now people this administration—and particularly the defense department."[12] Of the twenty-five founding members of the Project for the New American Century calling for "revolutionary changes" to make the world safe for America, almost all are now in high positions in the Pentagon and the White House.

Iran, as well as Iraq and Syria, features prominently in neoconservative concerns. In their eyes, the 1979 Iranian revolution turned politics upside down. In one swift blow, it wiped out their "island of stability" in the region, their main "policeman" in the Gulf, their major customer of high-tech military hardware, their main recycler of petrodollars, their second-largest provider of reliable and relatively inexpensive oil, and last, but not least, Israel's valuable ally in the hostile Muslim world. In other words, the revolution, in one swift blow, destroyed the famous Nixon doctrine that had appointed the shah to be the guardian of America's strategic as well as oil interests in the Gulf. In Kissinger's words, the shah supported the United States on virtually every major foreign policy issue. In return, the United States gave the shah "everything he wanted"—including help in starting a nuclear program.[13] The neoconservatives have made no secret of their desire to undo the 1979 revolution.

The 1979 revolutionaries added insult to injury by flagrantly humiliating the United States—by taking over its embassy as a "den of spies," accusing it of plotting a repeat performance of the 1953 coup, turning a rescue mission into a much publicized military fiasco, denouncing America as "Satanic," holding fifty-three of its citizens hostage for 444 days, and, to top it all, taunting the United States by proclaiming that it was too much of a paper tiger to be able to do "a damn thing." One should not overlook Occidental sensitivity over "losing face." In recent years such sensitivities have cropped up in the most unlikely places. For example, Bill Keller, the executive editor of the *New York Times*, admitted after the fall of Baghdad that he had supported the invasion of Iraq because Saddam Hussein had "brazenly defied us and made us seem weak and vulnerable, an impression we can ill afford."[14] If Saddam Hussein, who was willing to open up his palaces, was "brazen," one shudders to think how Americans perceive the Islamic Republic. If liberals consider Saddam Hussein "brazen," one can measure the hostility with which neoconservatives view Iran.

Immediately after the revolution, prominent neoconservatives raised the hue and cry "Who Lost Iran?" "The U.S.," according to Michael Ledeen of the American Enterprise Institute, "had lost a country of enormous strategic importance" because of failure of will in the Democratic administration and because of President Carter's misplaced concern about human rights. "The flood," he insisted, could have been stemmed if the United States had stood firm behind the shah and permitted him to use an "iron fist" against fanatics opposing "liberal reforms."[15] The whole discourse was reminiscent of the McCarthyist campaign "Who Lost China?" The main lesson Ledeen drew from the revolution was that the United States could prevent similar debacles in the future if it had "clarity of purpose and the resolution of mind and of the heart." This clarity was soon seen when Ledeen, as a consultant to Reagan's Pentagon and National Security Council, helped Col. Oliver North engineer the famous Iran-Contra deal. In later years, Ledeen attained easy access both to Richard Perle, the chairman of the powerful Defense Policy Board at the Pentagon, and to Karl Rove, President George W. Bush's closest advisor in the White House. Ledeen had first appeared on the public scene in 1981 when he had promoted the theory that Moscow had hired a Turkish fascist to assassinate the pope. His long résumé includes supporting the Angolan UNITA, writing for the right-wing paper *Il Giornale Nuovo*, and helping establish the Jewish Institute for National Security Affairs in Washington. The *Financial Times* described him as a go-between for Israeli lobbyists in Washington and Reza Pahlavi, who hoped to be restored to the Peacock Throne.[16] Ledeen can also be described as the neoconservative informal spokesman on Iran. He articulates in public views many of his colleagues prefer to keep behind closed doors. Soon after the fall of Saddam Hussein, he forthrightly stated that to win the war against "terrorism" and to "bring stability to Iraq" as well as to the rest of the Middle East, the United States had to "liberate Iran, at a minimum." "To leave the mullahs in power would be terrible." He added that Iran was like the Godfather running international terrorism: "There will never be peace until the mullahs are brought down in Iran," and that requires us—and other "civilized countries"—to understand the stakes and "call for regime change in Iran."[17]

Zalmay Khalilzad, another prominent neoconservative who published a book on the Islamic Republic soon after the revolution, wrote the new regime was both a "fundamentalist autocracy" opposed to Westernization and a "totalitarian one-party state" modeled on fascism and communism.[18] He considered it to be highly dangerous on the grounds that it wanted to export the revolution and generate the dynamics for permanent revolution against the United States. Thus the neoconservative antipathy to Iran reaches back to the very inception of the Islamic Republic. In the words of the *Weekly Standard*, a must-read for White House officials, America has a "blood debt" to repay against Iran going back to its ways of previous decades.[19] As a 1994 book from the Carnegie Endowment stated, these hawks— described as Expanded Confrontationalists—felt that "no accommodation should be attempted with the regime" and that "nothing short of its demise would serve Western interests." "These advocates insist that regimes such as the Islamic Republic are anathema to Western interests and to the new world order. A hard-line policy sets clear guidelines for executive and legislative action, and it might also give a strong boost to opposition groups and stimulate further dissidence within Iran."[20] These "confrontationalists" scored a major Senate victory in 1996 when they further tightened the economic sanctions that had been imposed in 1979. American companies were barred from importing petroleum from Iran, building pipelines there, and investing more than $20 billion there in oil and gas ventures. They tried to extend this embargo to European and Japanese companies, but the European Union threatened to sue the United States in the World Trade Organization. Senators favoring sanctions claimed— without a shred of evidence—that Iran had been behind the 1993 bombing of the World Trade Center.

Since then the neoconservative antipathy for Iran has grown by leaps and bounds. By 2002–2003, the joke making the rounds in Washington was: "Everyone wants to go to Baghdad; real men want to go to Tehran." Ledeen, who with former members of the fallen regime had established the Coalition for Democracy in Iran, was openly boasting that he could bring down the regime with a mere $20 million. "Time for diplomacy is over; it is time for a free Iran." He wrote on behalf of the concept of "total war," and praised Machiavelli for realizing that violent change is the essence of human history. "Creative destruction is our middle name." He describes Iran as the "mother of modern terrorism," and argues that "if it was taken out, militant groups opposed to Israel, like Hezbollah and Jihad, would lose their strongest foreign backer."[21] His coalition, which enjoys good relations with the American Israel Political Affairs Committee, echoes Ariel Sharon's call that Iran should be "liberated the day after Iraq is crushed."[22]

Meanwhile, William Kristol—editor of the *Weekly Standard* and founder of the Project for the New American Century—used Churchillian rhetoric on how "we are in a death struggle with Iran" and "must take the fight there, with measures ranging from public diplomacy to covert operations."[23] He advocated strong action and claimed that absence of such action in the past had resulted in "contempt and lack of awe for the U.S. in the Middle East. This has encouraged the rise of terrorist organizations."[24] Fouad Ajami, a rare Middle East expert who favored invading Iraq, self-assuredly told readers of the *Wall Street Journal* that the downfall of Saddam Hussein would inevitably lead to the collapse of the Islamic Republic.[25] James Woolsey, a former CIA director who had recently joined the neoconservatives, declared that the United States had now entered World War IV—the third being the Cold War—and that Iran would be one of its main antagonists.[26] "As we move towards a new Middle East, over the years, I think, over the decades to come, we will make a lot of people very nervous." He emphasizes that Iran is a "fanatical theocratic totalitarian state . . . ripe for the ash-heap of history."[27]

Perle, who as a consultant to Likud had opposed the Oslo Accords, boasted that events in Iraq would automatically lead to the collapse of the Iranian regime, and, thus, pave the way for peace and democracy throughout the Middle East. He had gone on record as stating "that the U.S. should do everything to encourage the centrifugal forces in Iran that, with any luck, will drive that miserable government from office."[28] Douglas Feith, the undersecretary of defense who had also advised Likud, bragged that the administration had "plans to remake the Middle East" and "create a new international way of thinking," and that an integral part of this plan was the removal of the "corrupt and unpopular regime in Iran."[29] On the eve of the invasion of Iraq, the Israeli defense minister flew to Washington to stress that Tehran was as "dangerous" if not more dangerous than Baghdad,

and had to be dealt with "diplomatically or militarily."[30] Bernard
Lewis, whom Paul Wolfowitz, the deputy defense secretary,
hailed as "a great scholar of the Middle East," claimed that Iranians, like all Middle Easterners, respect power, force, and tough-
ness. Besides, Lewis added, once we have invaded Iraq then
Iranians would beseech us, "Come this way please."[31] Members
of the Washington Institute for Near East Policy, a spin-off from
the American Israel Public Affairs Committee, claimed that democracy in Iraq would bring democratic change in Iran, and this
in turn would bring an "interminable decline in Islam."[32]

An Iranian exile residing at the Hoover Institution assured
Americans that regime change in his country—unlike in Iraq—
would automatically produce democracy because it had a large,
vibrant, and vital middle class.[33] This was reminiscent of the arguments used for invading Iraq. In fact, on the eve of that invasion Wolfowitz had told audiences that it would be easy to
introduce democracy into Iraq because that country had no history of ethnic conflicts and instead had a "large educated public."[34] Another exile claiming to represent the National Revival
Movement of Southern Azerbaijan boasted that he had had more
than fifty meetings with Washington officials—including members of the administration.[35] He added that he was forming a
common front with other ethnic groups, especially Baluchis, Arabs, Kurds, and Turkmens. An intelligence officer claimed that
"poking ethnic issues could bring down the whole regime in a
spectacular fashion."[36] This was the first time that Washington
had resorted to the "ethnic card" in Iran. During the Cold War,
the United States had always supported the central government;
the Soviet Union had at times been tempted by separatist movements.

At a conference entitled "The Future of Iran: Mullahcracy,
Democracy, and the War on Terror," organized by the American
Enterprise Institute, the Hudson Institute, and the Foundation

for the Defense of Democracies, well-known figures in Washington called for regime change in Iran.[37] Meyrav Wurmser of the Hudson Institute and the Likud-leaning Middle East Forum insisted that any talks with the "terror regime" in Tehran would be seen there as sign of American weakness. Her husband, David Wurmser, special advisor to the vice president, had earlier served under Netanyahu and had co-authored with Perle the famous paper, "A Clean Break," advocating the restructuring of the Middle East and the scrapping of the Oslo Accords. Another lead speaker at the conference, Uri Lubrani of the Israeli Defense Ministry, pontificated on how the "Irani mind" respects power and applauded the axis speech for signaling a "dramatic development" to Iran: "This spirit has to be continued and continued at an accelerated phase because time is now of essence." Morris Amitay of the Jewish Institute for National Security Affairs and of the American Israel Public Affairs Committee spoke in favor of "regime change" in Iran and took the State Department to task for contemplating negotiations with Tehran. A Pahlavi spokesman promised his audience that a liberated Iran, with its population of 70 million, would once again provide Americans with excellent "business opportunities."

Similarly, a resolution introduced into Congress urged the administration to work for regime change in Iran and not to legitimize the regime through negotiations. The resolution described Iran as having "undermined the national security interests of the United States."[38] The senator sponsoring the resolution urged the government to fund the Iranian opposition. "Now is not the time," he said, "for timidity or for trying to win the favor of a regime that is going out of its way to cause us harm." Another much publicized resolution allocated $20 million to bring about changes in Iran both through covert actions and open propaganda. A member of the administration told the press that this allocation would be channeled to the Voice of America, Radio

Free Europe, and émigré networks to "add volume and reach" for exiles in America.[39] Some of the money also went to royalist stations located in California that beamed programs into Iran. Not surprisingly, many European correspondents reported that as soon as Baghdad fell the neoconservatives began beating the "drums of war" against Iran.[40] On the whole, their views ran along parallel lines to those of Likud, which saw Iran as a formidable foe capable of eradicating Israel. In the word of the Israeli chief of staff, "Iran is the problem since it wants to destroy Israel."[41]

Those most vocal for regime change raise the following four charges against Iran: financing and arming international terrorists, opposing the Arab-Israeli "peace process," violating democratic and human rights, and, in more recent years, developing nuclear weapons. In fact, the Senate resolution specifically accuses the "unelected regime" of carrying out mass executions and depriving citizens, especially women, of their human rights; opposing the peace process; helping al-Qaida, the Taliban, Hamas, Hezbollah, and other terrorists; and, last but not least, building weapons of mass destruction. Of these five, only the last deserves serious consideration. The other four can be considered polemical issues.

It is true that Iran in the 1980s was involved in international terrorism, especially in assassinating more than seventy dissidents in exile—one in the United States, the others mostly in Europe. But this form of abhorrent behavior—which, incidentally, was mostly ignored by the United States at the time—diminished in the late 1980s and ended entirely after President Khatami's election in 1997. Since then, Iran has continued to give limited support to Hezbollah in Lebanon, but few in the international community consider this to be a "terrorist" organization. Iran, like much of the international community, considers Hezbollah to be a legitimate Lebanese organization fighting against foreign forces within its own country. Suspicions that Iran has master-minded bombings in Saudi Arabia, Lebanon, Israel, and Argentina have been based not on hard evidence but on rumors often taken more seriously in the Pentagon than in the CIA and State Department. Much has been made of rumors that Iran had a hand in the Khobar Towers bombing in Saudi Arabia. But the recent publication of the memories of al-Zawahiri, the master-mind of this venture, shows this not to be true.[42] Similarly, the capture of the Palestinian ship *Karine,* which was full of arms, near the Israeli coast seemed to prove that Iran was smuggling weapons to Arafat. The whole case, however, fizzled out when the Israelis displayed the weapons with much fanfare but pre-vented international journalists from getting close enough to in-spect their markings.[43] What is more, the claim that Iran supports al-Qaida flies against all common sense since Iran armed the Northern Alliance against the Taliban and almost went to war against Afghanistan in 2000. This has not deterred neoconser-vatives from giving wide publicity to an Iranian "defector" who claimed that Tehran "played a direct role in September 11."[44] An American intelligence officer described this defector as a "fabri-cator of monumental proportions." Another argued that there was "no credible evidence" that Iran had taken the highly unlikely step of helping bin Laden. "The two," he stressed, "would make unlikely bedfellows."[45]

It is true that Iran has been a gross violator of human rights. But the human rights situation has markedly improved since 1989—especially after Khatami's election. So much so that in 1998 the UN disbanded the special committee it had set up in the early 1980s to monitor human rights in Iran. This, however, does not prevent neoconservatives from acting as if nothing has changed. In 2003, one prominent neoconservative participated with much fanfare in a memorial service organized by a well-funded Los Angeles group to mourn the mass execution of communist

prisoners—which had taken place in 1988. This seems like a classic
case of crocodile tears, especially since at the time few in the
United States had deemed these executions to be worthy of mention. In fact, the State Department had welcomed the initial arrest
of the same prisoners two decades earlier. Speakers at the memorial service denounced not only Khatami but also American
"economic interests" favoring "appeasement."[46] Michael Rubin,
who had just moved from the American Enterprise Institute to
the Iran-Iraq desk at the State Department—probably over the
objections of the secretary of state—thanked Ledeen for speaking
the truth. He argued that the 1988 massacres made a mockery of
Khatami's talk of "dialogue of civilizations."[47] The *Washington
Post* informed readers that "the 1988 massacres had claimed thousand of victims for their political or religious views or for refusing
to sign false confessions."[48] The paper did not venture to explain
why it had taken it a full fourteen years to discover these massacres. The issue of human rights is especially problematic if one
remembers that the same neoconservatives, led by Elliot Abrams,
head of Middle East policy in the National Security Council;
John Bolton, undersecretary of state for arms control; John Ne-
groponte, the U.S. ambassador to the UN; and Otto Reich, another undersecretary of state, had done their very best in the
1980s to cover up the activities of death squads in Central and
Southern America. The Iranian regime, however bloody, is relatively benign compared to these death squads.

It is also true that Iran initially denounced the Oslo Accords
and opposed the two-state solution for Palestine. But since then
President Khatami has often gone on record as willing to accept
any agreement palatable to the Palestinians—even the two-state
solution with its implicit recognition of Israel. Iran obviously
does not want to give the appearance that it wants to fight Israel
to the very last Palestinian. Even the Leader has gone on record
as admitting that Palestine is "not Iran's Jihad." Besides, Iran has

little influence in the distant Mediterranean. Its connections with
Hamas and Jihad are indirect, tenuous, and insignificant. Moreover, the charge that Iran is sabotaging Oslo became obsolete if
not absurd once the Intifada restarted in September 2000, and
Likud, which had always opposed Oslo, returned triumphantly
to power. Iran cannot be accused of sabotaging a nonexistent
peace process. The neoconservatives who had opposed Oslo are
now denouncing Iran for not supporting the same Oslo. In polite
circles this is considered "ironic."

While these loaded and sensitive accusations can be dismissed
as mostly polemical and peripheral, the issue of nuclear weapons
remains real even though experts could debate its immediacy, and
those familiar with long-standing neoconservative aims could
question its centrality to their antagonism to Iran. The issue is
real enough to complicate relationships not only between Iran
and the United States but also between conservatives and neoconservatives in Washington, between Washington and its European allies, and between reformers and die-hard conservatives
in Tehran. In fact, the issue threatens to become entangled in the
mesh of the ongoing political struggles within Iran. In the words
of *Le Monde Diplomatique*: "A confrontation between Iran and
United States is definitely a possibility in the next few months or
after the forthcoming election, unless Washington changes its
tune."[49]

IRANIAN POLITICS

The conflict between reformers and conservatives is rooted in the
very structure of the Islamic Republic. The written constitution,
drawn up under Ayatollah Khomeini's supervision immediately
after the 1979 revolution and amended right after his death in
1989, tried to synthesize theocracy with democracy, divine right
with human rights, vox dei with vox populi, and clerical authority

with popular sovereignty. A constituent body, named the *Majles-e Khobregan* (Assembly of Experts) and chosen by the general electorate, attempted to merge Charles de Gaulle's Fifth Republic with Khomeini's concept of *Velayat-e Faqih* (Guardianship of the Clerical Jurist). According to this concept—expounded for the first time in 1970 through a series of public lectures known as *Velayat-e Faqih: Hokumat-e Islami* (Guardianship of the Clerical Jurist: Islamic Government), the clergy have the ultimate authority to supervise the state. After all, the state exists only to safeguard the *sharia* (divine law), and the clergy are the best qualified to understand, interpret, and implement the same sharia.[50] Nationwide referendums ratified both the constitution and the amendments totaling 177 clauses.

Before one jumps to the conclusion that the Islamic Republic is fatally flawed because of this contradiction, one should remember Isaiah Berlin's pertinent observation that liberal democracies manage to survive even though they espouse concurrently very different ideals—liberty and equality.[51] These two are not the same and can in fact work against each other. One can have a great deal of liberty but little equality. Conversely, one can have a great deal of equality but little liberty. Liberal democracies, however, manage by being flexible, sometimes favoring liberty at the expense of equality, at other times, equality at the expense of liberty. The Islamic Republic could possibly do the same moving back-and-forth between theocracy and democracy.

The constitution created a brand new rank titled the *Rahbar* (Leader). This was filled first by Khomeini, and upon his death by Ali Khamenei whom the state-media quickly elevated from the middle rank of *Hojjatalislam* (Proof of Islam) to the senior level of *Ayatollah* (Sign of God). According to the 1989 amendments, the Assembly of Experts can elect as Leader any cleric deemed "qualified," "worthy," and "suited."[52] The original constitution had stipulated that the Leader had to be a cleric of the highest

rank—an *Ayatollah-e Ozma* (Grand Ayatollah)—with impeccable
scholarly credentials in Islamic jurisprudence. Since none of the
senior ayatollahs subscribed to Khomeini's interpretation of
velayat-e faqih, his disciples had to settle on one of their own.
The Islamic Republic is known as the regime of ayatollahs. It
would be more apt to describe it that of hojjatalislams.

The Leader, according to the constitution, "determines the interests of Islam," "sets state guidelines," "supervises implementation of general policy," and, as the link between the three
branches of government, appoints an Expediency Council to me-
diate differences between the legislative, executive, and judiciary
branches. He can dismiss the president as well as vet candidates
for that office. As commander-in-chief of the armed forces, he
can convene the supreme military council, mobilize the troops,
declare war and peace, grant amnesty, and appoint the heads of
the army, navy, air force, and revolutionary guards. He can appoint and dismiss the chief judge, the state prosecutor, the revolutionary tribunals, and, through a separate law, the special
clerical court established to investigate the clergy. He can also
remove lower court judges. Even more important, he nominates
six clerics to the powerful twelve-man Guardian Council. This
council—more powerful than the U.S. Supreme Court—can veto
parliamentary bills on the grounds they run counter to the spirit
of either the sharia or the constitutional laws. This council has
also obtained—through a separate law—the power to supervise
elections and review candidates for elected office, including the
presidency and the *majles* (parliament).

Moreover, the Leader, through his pervasive influence through
the judiciary, was able to revamp the entire legal system. One of
Khomeini's very first decrees was to replace the Civil Law which
had been borrowed from Swiss Code with his sharia-inspired
Law of Retribution. This decree—supplemented with the Law of

Discretionary Punishments—codified the principle of an eye for an eye, a limb for a limb, a life for a life. They mandated death for "sowing corruption on earth," "declaring war on God," and "blaspheming against divinity." They reintroduced blood money as well as such corporal punishments as whipping and amputations. They separated victims, litigants, and witnesses into male and female, Muslims and non-Muslims. Evidence from Muslim males was worth twice that from Muslim women and non-Muslims. "Offenses against God"—apostasy, fornication, homosexuality, and habitual drinking—mandated hanging, stoning, or decapitation. Lesser offenses—such as theft, failure to wear proper "Islamic clothing," and socializing with members of the opposite sex—called for fines, flogging, amputation, or, as a concession to modernity, imprisonment. In homicide cases, relatives could participate in the actual execution, or, if they so preferred, accept monetary compensation. Khomeini also purged women from the judiciary and decreed that all lawyers and judges had to have proper seminary qualifications. What is more, family courts—headed by male sharia judges—reintroduced traditional rulings permitting men to divorce at will, removing restrictions on polygamy, favoring fathers in custody cases, and lowering the marriageable age for girls from sixteen to nine and boys from eighteen to fifteen.

The constitution also gave the Leader the authority to make a number of key appointments in semi-public institutions. These appointments included the city *imam jum'ehs* (Friday prayer leaders), the director of the national broadcasting service, the chairmen of the large religious endowments (the Foundations of the Oppressed, Martyrs, Housing, Pilgrims, and Publication of Imam Khomeini's Works), and the editors of *Kayhan* (The World) and *Ettela'at* (Information)—two long-established papers both owned by the Foundation of the Oppressed. These religious foundations grossed an annual income almost half that of the state budget.[53] Some consider these clerical fiefdoms to be states within the state.

The constitution, however, tempered theocracy with some important concessions to democracy. These concessions were incorporated in part because the revolution was carried out in the name of "liberty, equality, and social justice"; in part because the country had a long history of constitutional struggles going back to 1905—one of the main charges against the shah was that he had violated the 1905 constitution; in part because many secular organizations had participated in the 1979 revolution; and in part because the revolution had been carried out through street demonstrations, general strikes, and mass meetings. For many the 1979 revolution was the people in action. Thus the electorate—defined as all adults including women—had the authority to choose the Assembly of Experts as well as the president, the majles, and regional councils.

The president—elected every four years and limited to two terms—enjoys extensive authority. As the head of the executive branch, he chairs the cabinet and chooses all its members—with the exceptions of the minister of justice who is named in consultation with the chief judge, and the minister of intelligence, who according, to a separate law, has to be a cleric handpicked by the Leader. The president draws up annual budgets and supervises economic matters including the plan and budget organization. He is responsible for implementing the country's internal and external policies. He signs international treaties, laws, and agreements. He chairs the national security council. He appoints most senior civilian officials, including ambassadors, provincial governors, and town mayors. He also appoints directors to the large state organizations—the National Iranian Oil Company, the National Bank, and the National Electricity Board.

These public boards, together with the ministries, employ more than 700,000 civil servants and 1.7 million workers.

The majles—also chosen every four years through national elections—is enshrined in the constitution as "representing the whole nation." Initially it contained 270 seats and was elected by citizens over the age of fifteen. Now it contains 290 seats and is elected by citizens over the age of sixteen. It has the authority to investigate "all matters of state" and public complaints against the executive and the judiciary branches. It votes on annual budgets, government bills, foreign loans, and international agreements. It has the power to reject the president's choice of ministers and force their resignation through a vote of no-confidence. It chooses, from a list submitted by the chief judge, six of the twelve jurists for the Guardian Council. It can hold closed meetings, provide its members with immunity from arrest, and regulate its own internal working, especially debates and committee hearings. It determines ultimately whether a particular declaration of martial law is justified. It can legislate bills so long as they obtain the approval of the Guardian Council and are deemed to be *qanons* (statutes) not tampering with the sharia. The sharia comes from God; *qanons* can be made by the representatives of the people. What is more, the majles—with a two-thirds majority—can call for a national referendum to amend the constitution. This clause, passed without much fanfare, has turned out to be highly relevant in more recent years.

The regional councils hold out possibilities for grass-roots democracy. According to the constitution, the public can elect provincial, city, district, and even village councils. These councils, in turn, can oversee regional officials—governors, mayors, and village headmen—and supervise local cultural, educational, and social programs. This is important in regions inhabited by such ethnic minorities as Kurds, Baluchis, Turkmens, Arabs, and

Azerbaijanis. These councils, inspired by the Russian soviets, had first appeared in the 1905–1906 revolution. After a long hiatus, Khomeini had incorporated them into the constitution as a major concession to large demonstrations organized by the Left in 1979—by Marxists and the secular National Front as well as by the radical Mojahedin.

The constitution enumerated a long list of individual rights. It pledged to protect liberty, property, and security for all, "regardless of race, color, language, or creed." It guaranteed freedom of expression, thought, worship, publication, demonstration, and participation. It stated that people had the right to organize guilds, trade unions, professional associations, and political parties. It ensured "equal job opportunities," and "equality of men and women, before the law." It vowed protection from arbitrary detention, illegal searches, and police surveillance including wiretapping and arbitrary searches. It promised detainees indictments within twenty-four hours, and those accused of crimes fair and open trials, impartial juries, legal counsel, right of appeal, and the "presumption of innocence until proven guilty beyond any doubt." In reaction to well-publicized abuses during the former regime, the constitution proclaimed: "The use of force and physical torture to extract information or a confession is prohibited by law. Confessions obtained by compulsion through the use of torture are inadmissible evidence in a court of law. Any contravention of this principle is punishable by law." In short, the constitution implicitly incorporated the UN Declaration of Human Rights and the French Declaration of the Rights of Man and Citizen. It avoided, however, describing these "as natural rights." To have done so would have undermined the notion that all rights were derived from divinity.

The constitution also enumerated a long list of social and economic promises. It undertook to eradicate poverty and meet basic needs. It promised to provide employment, free education, free medical facilities, and such welfare programs as pensions, subsidized housing, unemployment pay, and disability compensation. It assured the ethnic minorities the right to have "their native languages used in the local press, media, and schools." It also assured the legally recognized religious minorities—Christian, Jews, and Zoroastrians, known collectively in Islam as the "People of the Book"—their own places of worship; their own community organizations, including schools; and their own marriage, divorce, and inheritance laws. These minorities, who constituted less than 1 percent of the total population, were allocated five majles seats: two for the Armenians, and one each for the Assyrians, Jews, and Zoroastrians.

The Islamic Republic, thus, is a mishmash of traditional theocracy and modern democracy. As the chair of the constituent assembly argued, since the vast majority of the people had participated in the revolution in the name of Islam then it followed that they favored a democracy confined within the boundaries of the sharia and the velayat-e faqih.[54] Ayatollah Hussein-Ali Montazeri, the assembly's formal president and for awhile Khomeini's designated successor, admitted in 1979 that if he had to pick between God and the voice of the people he would not hesitate in choosing the former.[55] Khomeini, however, on the eve of the referendum for the constitution, explained: "This constitution which the people will ratify in no way contracts democracy. Since the people love the clergy, have faith in the clergy, want to be guided by the clergy, it is only right that the supreme religious authority should oversee the work of the ministers and the president to ensure that they don't make mistakes or go against the Koran."[56]

This inherent tension remained hidden as long as the public supported the new regime; as long as the nation felt it was waging a life and death struggle against foreign invaders (the Iraqi war lasted from 1980 until 1988); and as long as Khomeini with his charisma was omnipresent. After all, he was hailed as the Leader of the Islamic Republic, Founder of the Islamic Republic, Guide for the Revolution, Supreme Jurist, Inspirer of the Oppressed Masses, and, most potent of all, Imam of the Muslim Community—in the past Iranian Shi'is had reserved this title, with its notion of sacred infallibility, for the lawful descendants of the Holy Prophet whom they termed the Twelve Imams. Khomeini was treated as if he had "charisma" in the true sense of the term—authority derived from God. Khomeini was able to keep his followers in line by setting guidelines and marking the parameters of public debate. He was also able to silence critical voices by simply denouncing them as enemies not only of the revolution and the republic but also of Islam and God. Such denunciations would prompt vigilantes, known as the *Hezbollah* (Party of God), to descend on dissidents, smashing bones, heads, offices, and printing presses. It did not take long to crush opposition from all spectrum of political life—from royalists on the Right, through secular nationalists in the center, all the way to Marxists and Maoists on the far Left.

The political climate, however, changed in the 1990s. The Iraqi war ended in 1988, terminating military mobilization and relaxing the public mood. The country no longer saw itself as facing mortal danger. Khomeini died in 1989 leaving behind a successor who lacked both his clerical authority and revolutionary charisma. Ayatollah Montazeri had been forced to resign as designated successor because of disputes over policies and interpretations of velayat-e faqih. According to Montazeri, the Leader was supposed to merely "supervise," not directly control, the administration of the Islamic Republic. What is more, years of war and revolution, compounded by a drastic decline in oil prices and an equally drastic rise in population, had generated a host of economic problems: unemployment, inflation, foreign-exchange crises, lack of investments, shortages of schools and housing, flight of capital and professionals, and continued influx of peasants into urban slums. These economic problems added to existing social tensions. These, in turn, eventually appeared in the public arena.

The changed political environment permitted the emergence of new voices—all with impeccable revolutionary credentials. They became known as the "religious intellectuals." Some had taken part in the struggle against the shah. Some had participated in the embassy takeover. Some had fought in the eight-year war. Abdul-Karim Soroush, the laureate of the new movement, is a chemist turned political philosopher who had helped purge the universities of non-Islamic elements. By the early 1990s he argued that Islam had become too "bloated" and needed to be cut down to its proper meaning—to personal ethics, piety, morality, and relationship to God. He likes to cite Kant, Hume, Locke, and Karl Popper's *Open Society and Its Enemies*.[57] For Soroush, the revolutionary environment of the 1960s to the 1980s had transformed Islam from religion into an ideology, like Marxism, claiming to have answers to everything including economics, society, politics, history, and, of course, jurisprudence. "The greatest pathology of religion I have noticed after the revolution is that it has become plump, even swollen. Many claims have been made in the name of religion and many burdens are put on its shoulders. It is neither possible nor desirable for religion, given its ultimate mission, to carry such a burden. This means purifying religion, making it lighter and more buoyant, in other words, rendering religion more slender by sifting, whittling away, erasing the superfluous layers off the face of religiosity."[58] He labels diehard conservatives as "monopolists," "fanatics," "right-wing extremists," *asoulgari* (fundamentalists), sunnatgari (traditionalists), mohafezeh-e kar (reactionaries), and even "Stalinists."

Similarly, Hojjatalislam Mohsen Kadivar, the main scholar who has scrutinized the concept of velayat-e faqih, began his revolutionary career as a seminary student in Qom. He argues that the concept is neither in the Koran, nor in the Prophet's *Hadiths* (traditions), nor in the teachings of the Twelve Imams.[59] He reminds readers that Khomeini had repeatedly promised the public a republic that would be democratic and similar to existing ones. "In a republic," Kadivar noted, "governors are responsible to the people. In velayat-e faqih the people are wards of the governors. . . . If the likes of our chief judge are true spokesmen of Islam then I am proud to be called an apostate."[60]

Saed Hajjarian, the movement's future strategist, had taken part in the embassy occupation and had served as deputy minister of intelligence until 1989. He had then set up through the foreign ministry a think-tank named the Center for Strategic Studies. Akbar Ganji, Ibrahim Nabavi, Mashallah Shamsolvaezin, and Hamid-Reza Jalaipour, were gadfly journalists who had fought in the war or had close relatives who had been killed in the front. Abbas Abdi, another gadfly journalist, had been one of the student hostage-takers. Ataollah Mohajerani, the future cultural minister, had been a majles deputy. Hojjatalislams Mohsen Saidzadeh, Abdollah Nouri, and Yousefi Eshkevari were young theologians who interpreted Islam to provide equality between men and women.[61] The first published *Freedom of Women in the Time of the Prophet*. Grand Ayatollah Youssef Sannei, a longtime aide to Khomeini and former Guardian Council member, even issued rulings that women had the right to hold any job including that of a judge, a president, and even Leader. He also argued that blood money should be equal; that first-trimester abortions be permitted if pregnancy threatened the mother's life or if the fetus was deformed; and that traditional laws should not be considered valid for all times and all places. These clerics can be described as supporters of Islamic feminism. Many of them had studied under Khomeini and Montazeri.

These new intellectuals aired their views through public lectures, books, pamphlets, quality journals such as *Kiyan*—named after a pre-Islamic Iranian dynasty, and, most important of all, mass-circulation newspapers: *Jameh* (Society), *Hayat-e Now* (New Life), *Hamshahri* (Fellow Townsman), *Iran*, *Bahar* (Spring), *Asr-e Azadegan* (Freeborn Age), *Zan* (Woman), *Azad* (Freedom), *Salam* (Greeting), *Mosharekat* (Participation), and *Neshat* (Joy). *Hayat-e Now*, edited by Khamenei's liberal brother, had a daily circulation of more than 235,000—double that of the long-established *Ettela'at*. Of course, the conservatives were also well armed with their own papers—*Kayhan*, *Jomhur-e Islami* (Islamic Republic), *Resalat* (Spiritual Message), and *Qods* (Jerusalem). Iranians dubbed this period the "years of press wars."[62]

These papers transformed the whole tenor of public debate. In the 1980s the key words had been *enqelab* (revolution), *emperyalism*, *shahid* (martyrdom), *jehad* (crusade), *mostazafin* (dispossessed), *mojahed* (fighter), *towhid* (monotheistic solidarity), *khish* (roots), *gharbzadegi* (western intoxication), and *seton-e panjom* (fifth column). In the 1990s the key terms became *demokrasi* (pluralism), *azadi* (freedom), *barabari* (equality), *moderniyat* (modernity), *jam'eh-e madani* (civil society), *hoquqi-e beshar* (human rights), *goft-e-gou* (dialogue), *moshkerat-e siyasi* (political participation), and the brand-new word *shahrvandi* (citizenship). Here was a cultural revolution as significant as the 1979 political revolution. Some papers such as *Asr-e Azadegan* published interviews arguing that the whole hostage crisis had been a major mistake. Ganji, the gadfly journalist, even raised questions about the validity of the whole sharia by pointing out that we have no real primary sources about the life of the Prophet.[63] This is probably the very first time in Iran that such radical skepticism had appeared in print.

The young movement crystallized into the Islamic Iran Participation Front. It soon won over prominent figures from the revolution—Hojjatalislam Mohammad Khoeiniha, the spiritual leader of the hostage-takers, Hojjatalislam Mehdi Karroubi, a close aide to Khomeini, and Hojjatalislam Hashemi Rafsanjani, the former president who now chairs the powerful Expediency Council. It also won over numerous Khomeinist organizations: the Society of Militant Clergy formed of theologians who wanted to distance themselves from the more conservative Association of Militant Clergy; the Mojahedin Organization of the Islamic Revolution created in 1979 to counter the antiregime Mojahedin; the Workers House with its trade unions and newspaper named *Kar va Kargar* (Work and Worker); and the Islamic Association of Students, Islamic Association of Women, Islamic Association of Teachers, Islamic Association of University Instructors, Islamic Association of Engineers, and Islamic Association of Doctors. The new movement was helped by older organizations— implicitly by the communist Tudeh Party and explicitly by the liberal Liberation Front. The latter had a licensed newspaper named *Iran-e Farda* (Tomorrow's Iran).

These organizations scored a series of impressive electoral victories. In July 1996, Khatami, the reform candidate, won the presidency with more than 70 percent of the vote in a campaign where nearly 80 percent of the electorate participated. He campaigned on the theme of civil society, rule of law, individual freedoms, women's rights, political pluralism, and "dialogue of civilizations." He stressed the need to "distinguish between real religion and traditions draped in religion," to borrow ideas of the Enlightenment, and to appreciate the beneficial aspects of the West. Khatami, a fifty-four-year-old hojjatalislam, had taught philosophy at Tehran University, headed the National Library, and served as cultural minister before being eased out for giving too much freedom to publishers, journalists, painters, and filmmakers. During his tenure the film industry had enjoyed a renaissance; the number of licensed journals had increased from 100 to 501, and that of book titles from 500,000 to more than 860,000. In his resignation letter he had warned that censorship would create a "stagnant and retrograde climate" which in turn would condemn the "nation's intellectuals, artists, and even faithful friends of the revolution to indifference."[64] His own works cited Voltaire, Rousseau, Montesquieu, Locke, Kant, Descartes, and De Tocqueville. "The essence of Iranian history," he likes to stress, "is the struggle for democracy."[65]

His conservative rival was another hojjatalislam with a much longer political curriculum vitae. He was the speaker of the majles and had the endorsement of the establishment, including the majority of deputies and imam jum'ehs, the bazaars and their chambers of commerce, the main seminaries and religious foundations, and the national broadcasting service. He had gone on record as arguing that: "Our system obtains its legitimacy from God. The legitimacy of the system does not rest on the people. Those who claim that the legitimacy of the Leader rests on the people don't understand our constitution."[66] His supporters openly argued that elected bodies were not so important, that the Islamic Republic should eventually be transformed into a fully Islamic government, and that God really chooses the Leader, with the qualified clerics merely presenting to the public that divinely chosen Leader.

Khatami ran a populist campaign, giving daily interviews, meeting voters in the streets and supermarkets, talking about his favorite hobbies—soccer, swimming, and table tennis—riding on public buses, and driving his own small car. He told a women's journal he wished his wife would learn how to drive. After his victory, he announced that he did not want his photograph hung in government offices. On the eve of the election, the London *Economist* predicted a shoe-in for the conservative candidate.[67] Since Khatami's upset victory came in May (*Khordad*), the reform movement took the label Khordad Front and launched a newspaper named *Khordad*. Although Khatami's support cut across all regions, classes, and generations, it was strongest among women, youth, and university students. He even carried the rank and file among the revolutionary guards. An Arab expert on Iran estimated that the solid core of the conservative vote was restricted to less than 10 percent of the population.[68] A more realistic figure is probably 20 percent. The *New York Times* commented:

> It is a time of aspirations and uncertainties, of risk-taking and resistance in Iran. At the heart of the tensions is the complicated question of whether Mr. Khatami—the moderate-sounding Islamic cleric who trounced a rival supported by the religious establishment—can guide Iran toward a different course. . . . With the backing of 20 million of 29 million Iranian voters, President Khatami can claim a popular legitimacy unmatched by any leaders since Ayatollah Khomeini died in 1989. But in exercising power, he faces competition from the religious establishment, whose dominant role in politics has been constitutionally guaranteed since the revolution.[69]

The Washington neoconservatives, however, dismissed Khatami as an Iranian Gorbachev, and saw the elections as yet another proof of the regime's widespread unpopularity. Meanwhile, Thomas Friedman, who never tires of repeating that democracy would solve most problems of the Middle East, now pontificated that what Iranians really need and want is not a liberal Gorbachev but a hard-nosed Ayatollah Deng who would provide them with money, jobs, and cyber-cafés. "Ayatollah Deng. You are needed in Iran."[70]

The Khordad Front scored another victory in the 2000 majles elections. They increased their support by over one million votes, collecting nearly 80 percent of the electorate, and winning 195 parliamentary seats. More than 5,800 candidates competed for the 290 seats. In Tehran, 861 competed for 30 seats. Dr. Muhammad-Reza Khatami, the president's brother, who edited the paper *Moshakerat* and had created the Islamic Iran Participation Party, topped the Tehran winners. The conservatives campaigned under the banner "Followers of the Imam and the Leader" but many of them, despite prestigious positions, failed to get elected even from their provincial hometowns. Even Qom, the country's religious capital, voted overwhelmingly for the reform slate. The London *Economist* wrote: "Iran, although an Islamic state, imbued with religion and religious symbolism, is an increasingly anticlerical country. In a sense, Iran resembles some Roman Catholic countries where religion is taken for granted, without public display, and with ambiguous feelings toward the clergy. Iranians tend to mock their mullahs, making mild little jokes about them; they certainly want them out of their bedrooms. In particular, they dislike their political clergy."[71] The *Economist* also reported that clerics complain that less than 1.25 percent of the population attend Friday prayer and 73 percent do not even say their daily prayers.[72] The reformers promptly followed up their parliamentary elections, by gaining control over the majles committees, electing Karroubi as speaker of the house, and forming a cabinet more to Khatami's liking.

The Khordad Front scored two additional electoral victories in the following year. They got Khatami reelected with a larger majority, increasing their vote by two million. They also swept the first nationwide local elections, winning 75 percent of the vote. More than 334,000 candidates, including 5,000 women, competed for the 115,000 town and village council seats. They also won all of Tehran's 15 seats. Their Tehran slate was led by Nouri and Hajjarian. In his electoral campaign, Nouri declared that "our Islam is that of love and friendship, not of suspicion," and that "we do not support a clerical leadership that would permit violence and breaking up of lawful meetings."[73] Thus by 2002 the reformers controlled the legislative and the local assemblies as well as the executive and the presidency.

The conservatives, however, continue to have easy access to the Leader, control the judiciary, and carry much weight in the military, especially among the intelligence services and the revolutionary guard officers. This has paved the way for a bitter tug-of-war—some would call it political guerrilla warfare. On one side, the conservatives can stymie the reformers by vetoing their legislation, closing down their newspapers, and citing the theocratic features of the constitution. The chief judge declared: "The Leader should be guided only by the Koran, the Hadiths, and the Prophet's teachings. The vote of the people can not over rule the representative of the Prophet."[74] These conservatives would endorse wholeheartedly nineteenth-century papal encyclicals denouncing popular sovereignty, natural rights, modernity, liberalism, and secularism as "heresies."

On the other side, the reformers counter by referring to the democratic features of the constitution, passing liberal legislations, and hoping that public pressure will eventually overwhelm their opponents. They hope that the weight of public opinion will demoralize some conservatives, win over others, and, at the same time, convince the Leader that the Islamic Republic will lose legitimacy if it refuses to listen to the voice of the people. As Khatami never tires of warning: "Only the people can ensure the long-term survival of the Islamic Republic." He also warns of the dangers of "religious fascism." The reformers stress that lack of reform will incite student and working-class demonstrations, creating instability, and thereby prompting the armed forces to carry out a typical military coup—but in the name of religion. The Islamic Republic could turn into an Islam State discarding its democratic features and becoming a fully theocratic one.

Initially Khatami scored a number of well-publicized political successes. He followed up his CNN appearance with numerous conciliatory interviews with Western reporters. He defused the decade-old Rushdie affair by assuring the international community that Iran had "no intention to threaten the author"; Britain, in return, restored full diplomatic relations. Khatemi also visited a number of foreign capitals—Moscow, Tokyo, Rome, Madrid, and Paris. At the Pantheon he laid wreaths for Rousseau, Zola, and Victor Hugo. He also quietly relaxed the heavy hand placed on the Bahai community ever since 1979 thereby gaining some begrudging praise from the State Department.[75] In the eyes of the conservatives, the Bahais were a heretical sect endangering the very existence of Shi'i Islam.

Khatami placed his supporters in the key ministries. His interior minister encouraged the newly created Human Rights Commission and sent a parliamentary commission to investigate the main prisons. The labor minister, who had been the chair of the Workers House, reaffirmed the government's commitment to the progressive Labor Law. The cultural minister issued some 200 new licenses, and encouraged the book and film industries. As a symbolic but significant act, he reinstated Oil Nationalization Day as a public holiday, and designated Mossadeq's home as a national heritage sight. For Nowruz—the pre-Islamic New Year, the minister issued special stamps, and permitted bonfires, fireworks, and street celebrations. Some conservatives view Nowruz as a "pagan" festival. The justice minister markedly improved prison conditions by removing a prison warden notorious for his cruelty. He also appointed women judges to family courts for the first time since 1979 and encouraged judges to shun physical punishments in favor of fines and prison sentences. Liberal newspapers, notably *Hayat-e Now*, argued that such public displays were detrimental to the country's image abroad. Besides, they added, they did not seem to deter criminals. The intelligence minister purged his officers: one for wanting to "cut out liberal tongues," others for belonging to a "rogue and out-of-control group" that had assassinated six secular intellectuals in the previous eight years—these murders were known as the "serial killings." The leader of this death squad conveniently committed "suicide" while in prison. Khatami praised this purge as the "removal of a cancerous tumor."[76] Khatami also persuaded the Leader to merge the revolutionary guards with the regular armed forces, and place them all under the defense minister. Meanwhile, the *basij*—which had been formed during the war as youthful reinforcements for the revolutionary guards—were instructed not to harass the public over dress codes, hair styles, videos, music cassettes, satellite dishes, Internet cafés, and private parties. The authorities were even instructed to arrest rowdy *hezbollahis*. As one party-goer said: "Before when we heard the doorbell we used to freeze in fear. Now we know someone is late."[77]

Khatami supporters passed over fifty reform bills. Most were vetoed by the Guardian Council; a few were watered down and then passed into law by the Expediency Council. The bills proposed a special press court outside the judiciary to give newspaper editors greater safeguards. They extended the teaching of English from secondary to primary schools. They reiterated the constitutional ban on torture and spelled out the forms of pressure that could not be used—blindfolding, sleep deprivation, solitary confinement, and lack of contact with family. This bill declared that detainees had the right to "counsel," "to be respected," be tried by judges with at least ten years experience, and have their family members immediately informed of their place of detention. The reform papers complained that prisoners who "confessed" were invariably given open trials but those who did not were inevitably tried in closed sessions.

The reform bills tried to whittle down the electoral power of the Guardian Council—candidates could swear allegiance to the

Islamic Republic rather than to the velayat-e faqih, and could be barred only if the Guardian Council gave written reasons. They tried to shift the authority to supervise elections from the Guardian Council to the Interior Ministry. They tried to introduce the jury system promised by the constitution; separate the function of prosecutors from that of judges; allow the president to suspend runaway judges; and eliminate the distinction between Muslims and non-Muslims, men and women, in accepting witnesses and awarding monetary compensation. They reactivated the parliamentary committee on women's affairs, gave state scholarships to women to study abroad, permitted deputies to wear *hejabs* (head scarves) instead of *chadours* (full covering), allowed schoolgirls to dress in bright colors, raised the marriageable age of girls from nine to fifteen (the Expediency Council eventually settled on thirteen), proposed giving women equal rights in divorce cases (even the right to initiate divorce), and extended divorced mothers' custody rights over sons from the conventional two years to seven. They tried to ratify—unsuccessfully—the UN Declaration on All Forms of Discrimination against Women (Iran and the United States have the distinction of being among the few countries that have not accepted this declaration). The reformers also gave government seed money to political parties to nourish civil society, and established a parliamentary committee to review foreign policy and find ways to improve relations with the United States. What is more, 100 deputies, together with 554 clerics, signed a petition requesting the release of Ayatollah Montazeri from house imprisonment. Some even called for the abolition of the Special Clerical Court on the grounds that the constitution did not mention such a body.

The conservatives fought back. The Guardian Council vetoed most of these reform bills, including the crucial ones on elections, courts, women, and press freedom. The courts closed down twenty-three dailies, including *Jameh, Neshat, Zan, Hayat-e Now,* and *Asr-e Azadegan*. This became known as the "great newspaper massacre." *Neshat* was closed down for favoring the abolition of capital punishment. This was seen as questioning of the sharia. *Zan* was banned for a cartoon which showed a husband trying to persuade a mugger to shoot his wife rather than him with the argument that her blood money would be "only half his." *Hayat-e Now*, edited by the liberal brother of the Leader, was suspended for reprinting a 1937 American cartoon which depicted Roosevelt's finger pressing down on a white-bearded Supreme Court judge who opposed the New Deal. Despite these closures, new publications and paper kept appearing with their total circulation tripling.[78] Meanwhile, the chief judge challenged the majles on its right of immunity. He accused five deputies of unjustly criticizing the judiciary, and thereby overstepping their constitutional rights. "The violence of the pen," he claimed, "is more lethal than that of the sword."[79] In this crisis over parliamentary immunity, the Leader sided with the majles to forestall a walkout by the vast majority of the deputies.

The courts, however, continued to accuse reformers such as Shamsolvaezin, Abdi, and Ganji, of undermining the republic. Abdi was imprisoned for releasing a public opinion survey which showed that 74 percent of the population wanted the government to enter negotiations with the United States. The same poll showed that 70 percent considered the Bush administration as highly "unreliable," and 66 percent still felt that the Islamic Republic could be reformed through the political process.[80] The chief judge ruled that newspapers were not allowed to advocate improved relations with the United States. The courts also accused the minister of oil and the popular mayor of Tehran of financial irregularities. The Special Clerical Court charged Kadivar, Eshkevari, Mohajerani, and Nouri of "blaspheming" and "questioning the concept of velayat-e faqih." Eshkevari was arrested after telling a human rights conference in Berlin that the veil originated not in Islam but in ancient Middle Eastern cultures. A history professor from the Khordad Front was taken to task for arguing that Iran desperately needed a Protestant Reformation. Sixty members of the Liberation Movement were put on trial for "undermining national security and propagating false information." Vigilantes disrupted public lectures given by prominent reformers such as Soroush. Armed men tried to kill Hajjarian, wounding him seriously. Some local judges continued to have video peddlers whipped in public. At times the police had to intervene to protect the lashers from the public.[81] A Shiraz court accused ten Jews and three Muslims of spying for Israel. This was clearly designed to sabotage Khatami's efforts to repair bridges to the West. Likewise, one of the religious foundations doubled the bounty offered to anyone who carried out the fatwa against Salman Rushdie. Ayatollah Hassan Saneii declared ominously: "The idea of Rushdie's annihilation is still much alive and seeks only the right moment."[82]

The conflict soon reached a stalemate. The conservatives could block reforms, close down papers, and put opponents on trial. The reformers, on the other hand, retained public support and even increased popularity as the other side became more intransigent and high-handed. For example, the trial of Nouri, the editor of *Khordad* and former vice president, became a major media event. The Special Clerical Court presented a forty-four-page indictment accusing him of apostasy, blasphemy, undermining the revolution, plotting to increase American influence, and subverting the Islamic Republic. He was also accused of publishing articles that challenged the sharia, especially over women's rights and the principle of an eye for an eye. American reporters drew parallels with the Scopes Trial; Iranians drew them with the medieval Inquisition. Nouri used the court as a platform to launch an assault on "political monopolists" who "hijacked the revolution and betrayed Khomeini." He challenged the legitimacy of the judge, reminding him that such a court did not exist in the constitutional laws. He exclaimed: "You can control tongues — even cut them off. But you cannot control minds or hearts." His defense speech, published as *Hemlock for a Reformer*, became an instant bestseller.[83] The first edition sold 50,000 copies in one week. The second edition sold 100,000 copies in the next two weeks. Fans even organized public book readings. The *New York Times* described the trial as a defining moment:

> . . . a moment when the courtroom becomes a testing ground for irreconcilable views about the future of society and its beliefs, with huge social, philosophical and political stakes resting on the outcome. . . . Mr. Nouri opened the key issue in the trial and to the wider political struggle across Iran: Whether power will be invested in the people, through the president and parliament they elect, or will continue to rest with a group of deeply conservative clerics who take their authority from Mr. Khomeini's successor.[84]

Even though the charges could not have been more serious, the judge — probably because of pressure from the Leader — sentenced Nouri to only five years. The trial ended with Nouri as a folk hero. The same is true of many others — especially Kadivar, Eshkevari, and Nabavi. Nabavi used his time in prison writing *Confession,* a biting satire in which he admitted to a host of crimes, including that of masterminding the recent serial killings.[85] He concluded by thanking Stalin for exploring the art of confession extractions, and his prison hosts for perfecting that art. *Confession* became as big a bestseller as *Hemlock for a Reformer*. By 2003, Nouri and Nabavi, as well as most of the others who were imprisoned, including Montazeri, had been freed. Even the Shiraz Jews were quietly pardoned or had their sentences drastically reduced. The saying in Tehran was "publish, then perish." But, in actual fact, the reformist intellectuals served short sentences and came out of prison better known than before. Upon his release from house imprisonment, Montazeri told journalists that governments should be democratic, clerics should keep out of daily politics, seminaries should be independent of the state, and the United States should cease giving unconditional support to Israel. He also criticized Khomeini for having prolonged both the hostage crisis and the Iraqi war.

The stalling of the reform movement caused much frustration. Khatami argued that the blocking of reform would lead to apathy, discontent, disillusionment, and, thereby, the undermining of the Islamic Republic. He warned that "fascists" and "reactionaries" were using religion to denounce their opponents as "Westernized liberals." He also hinted that he might resign and warned that "reforms have to be implemented slowly, step by step." Some supporters began to raise the possibility of amending the constitution through a referendum. Their main targets are the two most powerful instruments of the Guardian Council—that of vetting candidates and vetoing legislation. So far Khatami himself has shied away from mentioning the subject of referendum. He prefers to lobby with the Expediency Council and the Leader—he has weekly private meetings with the latter. The referendum, however, can always be used as a last card—especially since a recent public opinion poll showed that 94 percent want major reforms and 71 percent want a nationwide referendum.[86] In June 2003, 127 deputies sent an open letter to the Leader stressing that they, like many who had participated in the revolution and lost loved ones in the war, were deeply "anxious" that the "republic" was loosing "legitimacy" because "certain factions" were sabotaging the "reform program," instigating "crises every nine days," and making a mockery of electoral verdicts. "Given the current situation, we can conceive of only two alternatives:

either a fall into a dictatorship; or a rise into the democracy intended by the constitution. . . . We cannot claim that the Iraqi people should have the right to hold a referendum yet deny the same right for our own Iranian people."[87] It seems that the reformers' main hope is to increase their vote in the forthcoming parliamentary elections, due in February 2004, and then, armed with the needed two-thirds majles majority, call for a national referendum. Conversely, the conservatives intend to increase their seats by, on one hand, retaining their 10–20 percent of the electorate, and, on the other hand, creating a mood of disillusionment among the reformers, thereby drastically reducing overall voter participation. For the reformers, such a reduction would be tantamount to loss of legitimacy for the whole Islamic Republic.

Although the reformers failed to score major legislative victories, they achieved some successes in foreign policy and socioeconomic development. Relations with the European Union continued to improve after the resolution of the Rushdie affair. Khatami put a final end to assassinations of dissidents abroad. He invited delegations from the European Union and the UN to visit prisons. He assured them that the stoning clauses in the criminal law would not be put into actual practice. The European Union entered a "dialogue" with Iran linking human rights to economics, especially the prospects of new oil pipelines connecting Iran to the Mediterranean. Fifteen European countries decided not to introduce any motion critical of Iran at the UN Human Rights Commission while this dialogue continued. For the first time since 1979, the UN Human Rights Commission itself—in opposition to the United States—declined to take Iran to task. Iran also improved relations with Japan, Russia, Saudi Arabia, and almost every country except the United States. The Expediency Council, after overruling the Guardian Council, endorsed a new foreign investment bill permitting non-Iranians to own as much as 100 percent of companies in specific sectors of the economy. Under the shah, this had been limited to 49 percent. The government nurtured a stock exchange in Tehran, permitted the opening of private banks, and floated its first international bond. This was an instant success, attracting double the expected euros despite American opposition.

The World Bank and the International Finance Corporation—both overriding American opposition—loaned Iran over $500 million for development projects involving sewage works, water supply, and low-income housing. In previous years, Japan and the European countries had voted with the United States to block such loans. Having only 16.5 percent shares in the World Bank, the United States is in no position to prevent such decisions. This did not deter twenty-two congressmen from sponsoring a bill to prevent such World Bank loans and terminate all U.S.-Iran trade on the grounds that Iran was an "ideological dictatorship" and that the "pseudo-reformers" were no better than their rivals. What is more, European, Russian, and Japanese firms signed agreements to invest $12 billion in the oil, gas, and automobile industries. In the 1980s and 1990s, Iran had been considered one of the world's most inhospitable places for foreign investors. In 2002, it was rated by European and Japanese investors as safe. The European Union, however, while distancing itself from the hard-line U.S. policy, warned that relations would continue to improve only if Iran cooperated on issues of human rights, nuclear proliferation, and the Arab-Israeli dispute. The *Guardian* reported that "Europe showed its independence of the United States by agreeing to negotiate closer trade and political relations with Iran. . . . They also ignored energetic lobbying by Israel."[88]

The overall economic situation also improved. It improved in part because the Iraqi war had ended (the eight-year war had cost Iran over $70 billion and 700,000 lives); in part because less was being spent on the armed forces (under the shah the military had taken 17 percent of the gross national product but in 2002 it took less than 2 percent); in part because of a series of laws encouraging foreign investment and private banks, legalizing interest transactions and thus breaking usury taboos, denationalizing some industries, cutting subsidies to the religious foundations, unifying the foreign exchange system, and revitalizing the Tehran stock exchange; and, in largest part, because of the rise in world petroleum prices—the price of a barrel of oil rose from $10 in 1998 to $27 in 2000, and further to $30 in 2003. Oil revenues jumped from less than $10 billion in 1998 to $28 billion in 2001, and to over $30 billion in 2002. Foreign reserves rose to $4.8 billion, eliminating a $30 billion external debt, stabilizing the currency, and improving the country's creditworthiness. Iran became one of the few countries to have no foreign debt. It even set aside a nest egg for leaner years. The exchange rate was unified, depriving the religious foundations of artificially low-priced dollars. The gross national product grew 6 percent in 2000, 5 percent in 2001, and 6.8 percent in 2002—the non-oil sector increased nearly 8 percent in 2002–2003. Tax revenues jumped 24 percent in 2002. The unemployment rate fell from 16 percent to 12.5 percent. Inflation was reduced from 30 percent per year throughout the war years to less than 13 percent in 2000. For the first time since 1979, capital flew into the country both from expatriates and from foreign investors. The International Monetary Fund—hardly a friend of the Islamic Republic—gave Iran high marks in 2002 for its economic growth and fiscal reforms.[89]

The social reforms were even more impressive building upon programs initiated after the revolution but left short of funds until the late 1990s. By the early 2000s, most villages, not to mention towns (which constituted 65 percent of the country's population), had electricity, schools, health clinics, roads, and running water. The UN estimates that 94 percent of the population now has access to health services and safe water. The literacy rate rose from less than 50 percent in 1977 to 84 percent in

2002. Among those between six and twenty-nine years of age, it was as high as 97 percent. The infant mortality rate fell from 104 per 1,000 in the mid-1970s to 25 in 2002. Life expectancy increased from fifty-five years to sixty-nine—one of the best in the Middle East. Population growth declined from 4 percent per annum in the late 1980s to 1.2 percent in 2003—mainly due to the establishment of women's health clinics and the distribution of birth control devices. The UN commended Iran for this dramatic success, and predicted that the fertility rate—the average number of children born to a woman in her lifetime—which had plummeted from seven to three in the previous decade would further drop to two by 2010.[90] In other words, Iran has solved its population problem. The government tried to preempt AIDS by distributing condoms, holding sex-education classes, and legalizing prostitution.

Meanwhile, the number of students enrolled in universities increased from 140,000 in 1978 to nearly 1,700,000 in 2002. Women made major strides in higher education. By 2003, women formed 63 percent of the incoming university students, 54 percent of all college students, 45 percent of doctors, 25 percent of government employees, and 13 percent of the general labor force. The Internet, introduced in the 1990s, spread quickly, reaching over two million users by 2003. The regime distributed over 630,000 hectares of confiscated land to peasants, and gave farmers more favorable prices, especially for wheat. By the early 2000s, most independent farmers had such consumer goods as radios, televisions, refrigerators, and pickup trucks. In fact, the number of registered vehicles throughout the country had increased from 27,000 in 1990 to nearly 3 million in 2000. The *Economist* wrote in 2003: "The car industry is stirring and Iranian-made Peugeots, Kias, and a homegrown model, the X7, are now joining the traffic jams."[91] On the whole, the average Iranian, especially workers and peasants, are better off than their parents had been before the Islamic Revolution. This may help explain why the student protests of 1999, 2000, and 2003—caused by the closing down of newspapers—did not spark off nationwide disturbances. Neoconservatives who relish writing obituaries of the Islamic Republic are ignoring basic socioeconomic facts. But who wants facts to get in the way of ideology?

NUCLEAR IRAN?

Immediately after the fall of Baghdad, the Bush administration intensified pressure on Tehran by accusing Iran of clandestinely but rapidly assembling nuclear bombs—bombs that could be used against neighbors as well as given to international terrorists. This pressure came via the UN International Atomic Energy Agency, which, in May 2003, after finding small traces of enriched weapon-grade uranium, asked Iran to sign a new protocol to the Nuclear Non-Proliferation Treaty. This protocol would give inspectors unfettered access to all nuclear-related facilities throughout Iran. The United States added that if Iran did not give a satisfactory reply it would refer the whole matter to the UN Security Council. This instigated a new full-blown crisis. It heated up the cold war between Washington and Tehran. It complicated American-European relations—relations already strained by the Iraq war. It further complicated the internal situation in Iran, weakening the reformers and strengthening the conservatives. It also complicated the situation closer to home in Washington, adding to tensions between neoconservatives in the Pentagon and the more traditional conservatives in the State Department. These parties have different ways of resolving the crisis. One party—probably the more powerful one in the long run—has the clear purpose of using it to bring about "regime change" in Iran. We may be heading for yet more "interesting times." In the words of *Le Monde Diplomatique*, "Iran is in danger of becoming, one way or another, another case for the application of the new U.S. doctrine of preemptive action."[92]

Iran's nuclear intentions are shrouded in mystery. This is not surprising. Few countries are in the habit of discussing their nuclear intentions in public. Moreover, nuclear programs, by their very nature, do not distinguish into civilian and military branches until late in the day when the country is ready to make the actual decision to assemble a bomb. Consequently, others can never be sure that a particular nuclear program will not later develop military capabilities. Thus a country can sign the Non-Proliferation Treaty but still renege when ready to make the final dash. In fact, the treaty permits countries to give a three-month notice of "withdrawal" if they decide that "extraordinary events have jeopardized their supreme interests." Iran began its nuclear program in the early 1970s when the shah claimed that he needed alternate sources of fuel for the day when the oil reserves would be depleted. The United States, Germany, and France signed contracts to build him twelve nuclear plants. He told Western journalists: "Without doubt, and sooner than you think, we will have nuclear arms."[93] Fortunately most of these projects were scuttled during the revolution and the subsequent war.

It was not until the 1990s that Iran revived a much more modest nuclear program. It contracted Russia—against American opposition—to finish a nuclear power plant in Bushire. It also started on its own—perhaps with a little help from China and India—two small facilities in Arak and Nantaz (near Kashan). They use locally mined uranium, and can produce both low-enriched uranium for light-water civilian fuel or highly enriched uranium for military weapons. It is thought that when these plants are completed at the end of the decade they could produce enough highly enriched uranium to make several nuclear bombs.[94] Intrusive inspections would ensure that they were producing only light-water fuel, not highly enriched uranium. In theory, Iran could open up the facility, abide with regulations, but years later legally withdraw from the Non-Proliferation Treaty and then produce heavily enriched uranium. The International Institute for Strategic Studies warned in early 2003: "If Iran carries on regardless in pursuing an enrichment capability, there is a risk that Washington may consider military options to destroy the facility—much as Israel destroyed the Osirak reactor in Iraq in 1981."[95]

While the European Union shares America's concerns, its members, including Britain, prefer to handle the problem through "dialogue," "critical engagement," and avoidance of the threat of force.[96] The Group of Eight Developed Countries jointly stated: "We urge Iran to sign and implement an IAEA Additional Protocol without delay or conditions. We offer our strongest support to comprehensive IAEA examination of this country's nuclear program."[97] The EU told Iran that their entire relationship, including economic ties, would be jeopardized if Tehran was not forthcoming. It warned Iran that it must accept tougher inspectors if it is to convince doubters it is not developing banned weapons. The French foreign minister weighed in with the blunt warning that Iran faced a "strategic choice."[98] Meanwhile, a British official told reporters that "his government did not share Washington's view that isolation is the best way to deal with a regime characterized by a power struggle between reformists and conservatives. It is not clever to back people up against a wall to the point where they cannot acquiesce in what you are asking to do because it's become a trial of strength. But the Iranians are not going to get the trade deal without a political deal."[99] Some European governments may suspect that the crisis would not go away even if Tehran agreed to all the inspections. Washington's real concerns may rest elsewhere. An editorial in the *Guardian* argued: "Tehran should be brought into a regional dialogue on confidence building; the US should drop its objection to Iran joining the WTO and lift sanctions. Iran has to be reassured that it will be secure and regionally powerful without nuclear weapons. Current US hostility will only drive Iran further down the nuclear road, by reinforcing the most hard-line images of the Great Satan."[100]

The "axis of evil" speech, now compounded by the nuclear issue, has further complicated the conflict between reformers and conservatives in Iran. Of course, both have serious concerns about national security. Both know that they live in a "dangerous neighborhood"; that Pakistan, their strategic rival in Central Asia, has nuclear bombs; that Saudi Arabia has been talking about buying such bombs from Pakistan; that others, namely Russia, China, India, and Israel have large stockpiles; that for years influential voices in Washington and Tel Aviv have been calling for "regime change" in Iran; that they are now surrounded with American bases in Turkey, Georgia, Iraq, Uzbekistan, and Afghanistan; that atomic weapons provide national prestige and presumably entry into the "nuclear club"; that Iraq, a country without such weapons was invaded, but North Korea, a country with them, has not been; and that the ongoing instability in Iraq could easily overflow into Iran—they may remember Rumsfeld's motto "When you have a problem you can't solve, expand it." In the words of the *Guardian*, "Iran's fears are real": "Iran does have one deeply persuasive reason for acquiring nuclear weapons: national security. . . . Barely a week goes by without US officials making threatening noises towards Iran, decrying its alleged support of international terrorism, encouraging internal civil insurrection, or reminding it that like Iraq, the US deems it to be a rogue state."[101] Surprisingly, George Tenet, the CIA director, came to a similar conclusion when presenting his 2003 annual report to the Senate: "No Iranian government, regardless of its ideological leanings, is likely to abandon weapons of mass destruction seen as guaranteeing Iran's security."[102]

While reformers and conservatives share common concerns about national security, they differ in tactics—especially on how to deal with the United States. The reformers consider Europe—as well as Japan and Russia—to be vital bridges needed to bypass American efforts to isolate Iran. They are, therefore, more likely to be forthcoming on the issue of nuclear inspections, and be willing to slow down weapons programs in return for preserving good relations with the UN and the EU. They have agreed to more inspections, to consider the added protocols, and have reassured the UN that the nuclear program had no military component. Khatami assured diplomats that Iran had "no intention of getting nuclear weapons" and that the United States should not use this as a pretext and threat."[103] The EU, in turn, told Iran that it is willing to share nuclear technology if it is sure Tehran is not interested in nuclear weaponry. What is more, the reformers continue to openly warn the conservatives that the best safeguard against American subversion and another 1953 coup is to retain the confidence of the general public through an open society, free press, meaningful elections, and genuine mass participation. In short, they continue to insist that the Islamic Republic will not be secure until it has become fully democratic.

The conservatives, however, counter that any concession given on the nuclear issue will tempt the United States to demand yet more concessions on a host of other issues. As the spokesman for the Guardian Council argued, Iran should consider withdrawing from the Nuclear Non-Proliferation Treaty on the grounds that the new demands "humiliate Islam" and that many other countries, such as Israel, have never signed it, or, like North Korea, have withdrawn from it.[104] In addition, the conservatives continue to argue that further opening up of the political arena would provide the United States with a perfect opportunity to overthrow the Islamic Republic. In the words of the Leader: "We are not liberals, like Allende (and Mossadeq) who are willing to be snuffed out by the CIA."[105] Not surprisingly, the conservatives invariably cite national security when closing down papers, axing parliamentary candidates, arresting dissidents, using special courts, and depriving the accused of counsel, juries, and open trials. They have their own versions of the USA Patriot Acts I and II. "The conservatives," wrote one analyst, "were clearly on the defensive until President Bush came to their rescue by naming Iran as part of the 'axis of evil.' This threw the reformers on the defensive."[106] The correspondent for the *New York Times* reported after watching a march of millions denouncing the axis speech:

> Ever since Mr. Bush designated Iran part of the international terrorist network open to American attack, conservatives in Iran have been greatly buoyed, trying to use a resurgence of disgust with America to quash reform at home. This has made it hard for President Khatami to preserve his reformist agenda of promoting democracy and rooting out corruption—an agenda he emphasized today before he, too, criticized American foreign policy.[107]

Similarly, Jahangir Amuzegar, a rare senior official from the previous regime who keeps a balanced view of the new regime, wrote in *Foreign Affairs*:

> The unelected rulers whom Bush sought to condemn used the message to arouse public anger against the United States. Supreme Leader Ali Khamenei (who is backed by the hard-line fundamentalists), Khatami (who spearheads the elected reformers), and former president Hashem Rafsanjani (who leads the modern technocrats) joined together to denounce Bush's statement as interference in Iran's domestic affairs. Even

Ayatollah Taheri—a leading dissident who had chas-
tised the theocracy days earlier and was expected to
welcome U.S. support—joined the three in asking for
anti-American demonstrations. Indeed, many reformers, eager to prove their patriotic bona fides, were
more vehement than were conservatives in repudiat-
ing the White House's message. As a result of this
united front, government-sponsored demonstrations
in Tehran and other major cities became a forum for
a brand of virulent anti-Americanism rarely witnessed
during Khatami's presidency.[108]

Meanwhile in Washington, neoconservatives and more traditional conservatives continue to debate Iran. The former, entrenched in the Pentagon and to a lesser extent in the White
House, claim that there is no substantial difference between Iranian liberals and conservatives and that Khatami is merely a more
"humane" cover for Khomeini and Khamenei. In the past they
would have dismissed them all as "fundamentalists." But, having
recently formed an alliance with Pat Robertson, Ralph Reed, and
Jerry Falwell, they have dropped this loaded term. They also
claim that time is of the essence and Iran is on the verge of
building a nuclear bomb; that Iran is financing "terrorism" in
Iraq, Lebanon, Afghanistan, and Israel; that the regime is so unpopular that it is about to unravel—anecdotal reports are used to
support this contention; that the "liberation" of Iraq has boosted
the "democratic movement" in Iran; and that once the regime
unravels it will inevitably be supplanted with a fully secular democracy—just like the one promised in Iraq.

To hasten the arrival of such a democracy, the neoconservatives have patronized a strange assortment of bedfellows: mon-
archists eager to restore the Pahlavis; Mojahedin fighters whom
Saddam Hussein had armed and the Clinton administration had

placed on the terrorist list; aged Maoists who in 1981 had launched an aborted guerrilla war in the Caspian forests; Azeris separatists eager to join the Republic of Azerbaijan; and such recent defectors as Hussein Khomeini, the unknown grandson of the famous Khomeini. In September 2003, Ledeen brought Hussein Khomeini to the American Enterprise Institute where the latter told his audience just what they wanted to hear: that Iranians respected Bush as another Churchill, saw the hand of God in the "liberation of Iraq," thanked the administration for bringing "security" to Baghdad, hoped that the United States would pursue the struggle across the border, and invited the United States to invade Iran as soon as possible. In introducing his guest, Ledeen avoided mentioning that his grandfather had kept him out of politics because of his links to the Mojahedin.

The conventional conservatives, from their base in the State Department and to a lesser extent in the CIA, counter that Iran is not an imminent danger to the United States. They note that Iran lacks missiles capable of reaching the United States; that it needs years to develop an actual bomb; that inspections can further delay this; that the United States requires EU and UN cooperation to effectively pressure Iran; and that the regime is not about to unravel. They also have little patience with the opposition. Immediately after the fall of Baghdad, Colin Powell overruled strong objections from the neoconservatives and closed down Mojahedin bases in Iraq. Foreign correspondents in Washington note that officials from the State Department often remark that Iran is "not a pack of cards about to collapse," that internal discontent is not significant, and that an excessively hard line could both undermine the liberals and speed up the bomb.[109] The CIA went on record as predicting that the regime would "not implode but could evolve towards a more open government."[110] Such sentiments prompted Pat Robertson to declare that the State Department "threatened" U.S. security and that Foggy Bottom should be "nuked." The State Department was not amused. In October 2003, immediately after Iran agreed to permit UN inspections in exchange for European technical assistance for developing nuclear energy for peaceful purposes, Richard Armitage, the deputy secretary of state, informed the Senate that the United States was not working for a "change of regime" in Iran. The State Department felt that the deteriorating situation in Iraq necessitated cooperation with Tehran, and that "any government in Iran—even a secular one—would probably continue the quest for nuclear weapons."[111] Meanwhile, Anthony Cordesman, a former CIA analyst, told the Senate: "Labeling Iran as part of an 'axis of evil' is the worst possible way to influence the Iranian people. . . . I think our rhetoric on Iran illustrates a broad problem in American policy. We speak in terms of domestic politics to American audiences in ways which undermine our credibility in Iran, in the Middle East, in Europe, and in the rest of the world."[112]

The New York Times reported that people in Tehran treated talk of Pahlavi restoration as a bad Los Angeles joke.[113] The same paper added: "There are plenty of university students across Iran who will say in whispers that they hope Iran is next on America's democratization hit list. But delve a little deeper, and they'll admit it's a pipe dream—that no matter how much Iranians may hate the regime oppressing them, if they see American soldiers advancing across the Iranian border, they would take up arms to defend their soil and their history."[114] Another major American paper reported that Iranian liberals considered Bush's avowed support for democracy as tantamount to the kiss of death: "If America says the reformists are very good, or that the United States would protect us, this is very dangerous, because the conservatives will misuse it—to say we have secret relations with the American superpower, that we don't want Islam, that we would sell our country to someone else."[115] Similarly, the Brussels-based International Crisis Group reported that its extensive research in

Iran showed that the "long-entrenched contradiction between theocratic and democratic rule" was more likely to be resolved through internal gradual changes than through drastic externally driven forces.[116] The same message was conveyed by Shirin Ebadi, the Nobel Peace Prize winner, who, on her return to Tehran, told the press that the "age of revolution" was over, that there was no guarantee that another revolution would improve the situation, and that the "only way" forward was through peaceful reform.[117]

Geoffrey Kemp, a special assistant to President Reagan, warned: "U.S. talk of destabilizing the regime is dangerous. If the opportunity for cooperation is missed, the likelihood of an Iranian bomb will increase and, at an indeterminate time, a confrontation will materialize."[118] Gary Sick, a member of Carter's National Security Council, added:

> There are a lot of people in Washington seriously looking for a revolution on the cheap. They figure that by the U.S. simply making periodic statements, and with the LA stations broadcasting incendiary messages every night, that the people will rise up, overthrow the mullahs and replace them with a democratic government, and that basically we won't have to get our hands dirty at all. It's the equivalent of the cakewalk scenario for Iraq. It's an even more foolish analysis of what's likely to happen.[119]

A similar conclusion was drawn by Robert Malley, President Clinton's special assistant for the Middle East:

> One thing appears evident. A policy that depicts Iran as a part of an "axis of evil," lumps reformers and conservatives and banks on a popular uprising by the

Iranian people will at best be ineffective and at worst
will backfire. It is based on two faulty assumptions:
that conservatives have neutralized the reformers, and
that there is a clear divide between an entrenched and
uniform "regime," on the one hand, and a dissatisfied
populace, on the other. Yet, unlike the situation that
existed in the 1970s under the shah, the current regime
enjoys genuine support from considerable segments
of the population, including some who strongly object to its policies.[120]

In an unpredictable world, one can safely offer five general
predictions about U.S.-Iranian relations for the next few years.
First, the neoconservatives will continue to exercise considerable
influence in Washington, even if Bush loses in November 2004.
Their influence will remain strong in Congress, in the mass media, and in the policy-driven think tanks. Second, their hostility
toward Iran, whether through the White House or the Congress, will persist unabated and remain single-minded. Their ultimate aim is to undo the "loss" of Iran, negate the 1979
revolution, and thereby bring the country into the U.S. fold. It
is not for naught that neoconservatives describe themselves as
true "radicals." Third, an outright military invasion of Iran—
even if it had been tempting before the Iraqi debacle—is not on
the books for the foreseeable future, especially so long as Powell
and his State Department have some say in foreign policy. For
the more conventional conservatives, the United States has more
on its plate in Iraq than it can possibly digest, and Rumsfeld's
generous offer of "seats at the table" is clearly not attracting
would-be guests from the rest of the world. The "coalition of
the willing" remains the coalition of the taking. The neoconservatives would revisit the notion of a military invasion only if
Bush won in November, the Iraqi insurgence fizzled out—a

highly unlikely eventuality—or the international community stepped in to bail the United States out of Iraq—an even more unlikely eventuality since such help would merely give Washington the license to go into Iran and elsewhere. Fourth, U.S. hostility by itself is not going to bring down the Islamic Republic. The Iranian regime, despite its problems and weaknesses, is not a pack of cards perched to collapse because of much huffing and puffing in Washington and Los Angeles.

Finally, outright U.S. hostility, instead of weakening the regime, is more likely to strengthen the die-hard conservatives. The conservatives will use their American card to the hilt. They will continue to exclaim that the nation is in dire danger, the CIA is plotting another 1953, dissenters are a fifth column, state sovereignty should take priority over personal rights, and a new imperial power, far more powerful than the nineteenth-century ones, is at their doorstep hungry to devour the whole country. Such themes resonate well in a nation that has struggled for a hundred years to gain full independence from colonial powers. Some reformers will be won over. Some will practice self-censorship. Some will put the issue of reform on the back burner for the time being. If the reformers don't practice self-restraint, then the archconservatives may be tempted to carry out a coup and replace the Islamic Republic with a full Islamic state—an Imamate not very different from the Taliban-styled Emirate of Afghanistan. The net result will be either the further stalling or the absolute end of internal reform. U.S. foreign policy, invariably carried under the banner of spreading democracy, will once again end up undermining democracy. The twenty-first century may well turn out to be merely a continuation of the twentieth century—unless, of course, we have regime change in Washington.

NOTES

1. CNN, "Interview with President Khatami," January 8, 1998.
2. Secretary of State Madeleine Albright, "Address on Iran," *Iran Times*, March 24, 2000.
3. Elaine Sciolino and Nazila Fathi, "British Minister Meets Top Iranian," *New York Times*, September 26, 2001.
4. Nazila Fathi, "On the Sly, Iran Weighs Closer Ties with U.S.," *New York Times*, November 9, 2001.
5. Gary Sick, "The Axis of Evil: Origins and Policy Implications," *Middle East Economic Survey* 45, no. 14 (April 8, 2002).
6. President Bush, "State of the Union Message," *New York Times*, January 30, 2002.
7. Brian Urquhart, "World Order and Mr. Bush," *New York Review of Books*, October 9, 2003.
8. Arthur Schlesinger, "Eyeless in Iraq," *New York Review of Books*, October 23, 2003.
9. Hendrik Hertzberg, "Axis Praxis," *New Yorker*, January 13, 2003.
10. Sonni Efron, "Loyalists Say the Pentagon Is Usurping Foreign Policy," *Los Angeles Times*, May 8, 2003.
11. Sick, "The Axis of Evil."
12. Julian Berger, "Washington Diary," *Guardian Weekly*, October 16, 2003.

13. Frances FitzGerald, "Giving the Shah Everything He Wants," *Harper's*, November 1974, 55–82.

14. Bill Keller, "The Boys Who Cried Wolfowitz," *New York Times*, June 14, 2003.

15. Michael Ledeen and William Lewis, *Debacle: The American Failure in Iran* (New York: Vintage Books, 1982). See also Michael Ledeen and William Lewis, "Carter and the Fall of the Shah," *Washington Quarterly* 3, no. 2 (Spring 1980), 3–40.

16. Andrew Killgore, "Israel Lobby . . . ," *Washington Report on Middle East Affairs* 22, no. 6 (July 2003), 15.

17. Front Page, "Symposium: Jihad in Iraq," September 5, 2003, www.frontpage.com.

18. Zalmay Khalilzad and Cheryl Benard, *"The Government of God": Iran's Islamic Republic* (New York: Columbia University Press, 1984).

19. Tamara Wittes, "Quietly Rooting Against Saddam," *Weekly Standard*, April 7, 2003.

20. Geoffrey Kemp, *Forever Enemies? American Policy and the Islamic Republic of Iran* (Washington, DC: Carnegie Endowment, 1994), 12.

21. Mark Follman, "Is Iran Next?," www.salon.com.

22. *Guardian*, November 4, 2002.

23. William Kristol, "The End of the Beginning," *Weekly Standard*, May 12, 2003.

24. Guy Dinmore, "Bush ideologues reshape world over breakfast," *Financial Times*, May 22, 2003.

25. Fouad Ajami, "Iran Expects," *Wall Street Journal*, February 13, 2003.

26. Gerard Baker, "After Iraq, where will Bush go next?" *Financial Times*, April 14, 2003.

27. Jamie Glazov, "Iran, a Coming Revolution?," *Front Page Magazine*, September 18, 2002.

28. Amin Tarzi, "Proliferation Assessment," http://cns.miis.edu/pubs/opapers/op8/op8.pdf.

29. Nicholas Lemann, "After Iraq: The Plan to Remake the Middle East," *New Yorker*, February 17, 2003.

30. David Hirst, "Will Iran Be the Next Target?," *Daily Star*, January 25, 2002.

31. Bernard Lewis, "Time for Toppling," *Wall Street Journal*, September 28, 2002. See also interview with Professor Bernard Lewis, C-SPAN, December 30, 2001.

32. Carnegie Endowment, "Post-Saddam Mirage of Democracy."

33. Abbas Milani, "Can Iran Become a Democracy?," *Hoover Digest*, no. 2 (2003).

34. Melissa Block, interview with Paul Wolfowitz, National Public Radio, February 18, 2003.

35. BBC, "USA Sees Azeri Movement as Driving Force in Iran," *BBC Monitoring International Reports*, June 29, 2003.

36. Sharon Behn, "Pentagon Officials Meet with Regime Foe," *Washington Times*, June 4, 2003.

37. American Enterprise Institute, "The Future of Iran," www.aei.org/events/eventID.300/transcript.asp.

38. U.S. Congress, "Senate Resolution 306," www.mehr.org/resolution_306.

39. Mike Allen, "U.S. to Beam TV Show to Iran from Washington," *Washington Post*, July 3, 2003.

40. Andrew Stephen, "Washington hawks have turned their attention to Iran," *New Statesman*, June 6, 2003.

41. Aluf Benn, "Israel, U.S. remain ambivalent over Iran," *Haaretz*, January 22, 2002.

42. al-Zawahiri, *Knights under the Prophet's Banner* (original Arabic version serialized by *al-Sharq* in December 2001; English translation at www.fas.org/irp/world/para/ayam_bk.html).

43. Brian Whitaker, "Row over arms ship eclipses peace talks," *Guardian Weekly*, January 10, 2002.

44. Kenneth Timmerman, "Defector Says Iran Played Role in 9/11," *Insight Magazine*, June 12, 2003.

45. James Risen, "Bin Laden Sought Iran as an Ally," *New York Times*, December 31, 2001.

46. Mohammad Parvin, "Speech in Remembrance of the Prison Massacres," www.mehr@mehr.org.

47. Michael Rubin, "Speech to Mehr," www.mehr@mehr.org.

48. "In Prison, Iranian Found Solace in Art," *Washington Post*, October 2, 2002.

49. Paul-Marie De La Gorce, "Iran: the nuclear quest," *Le Monde Diplomatique*, October 2003.

50. Ayatollah Khomeini, *Velayat-e Faqih: Hokumat-e Islami* [Guardianship of the Clerical Jurist: Islamic Government] (Tehran: N.p., 1978).

51. Isaiah Berlin, *Four Essays on Liberty* (Oxford: Oxford University Press, 1975).

52. Central Office for Legal Matters, *Qanon-e Asasi-ye Jomhuri-ye Islami-ye Iran* [The Constitution of the Islamic Republic of Iran] (Tehran: Government Publishing House, 1989).

53. Jamshid Amuzegar, *Iran's Economy Under the Islamic Republic* (London: Taurus Press, 1994), 100.

54. See Ayatollah Muhammad Beheshti's speeches in Islamic Republic of Iran, *Surat-e Mashru-e Mozakerat-e Majles-e Barrasi-e Naha'iy-e Qanon-e Asasi-ye Iran* [The Complete Collection of the Final Debates of the Assembly for the Iranian Constitution], vol. 1 (Tehran: Government Publishing House, 1985).

55. Ayatollah Montazeri, *Ettela'at*, October 8, 1979.

56. Oriana Fallaci, "An Interview with Khomeini," *New York Times*, October 7, 1979.

57. Abdul-Karim Soroush, *Qabz va Bast-e Teorek-e Shariat* [The Expansion and Contraction of the Sharia Theory] (Tehran: Farhang Sirat Publication, 1990).

58. Abdul-Karim Soroush, *Reason, Freedom, and Democracy in Islam*, trans. Mahmoud and Ahmad Sadri (New York: Oxford University Press, 2000), 21.

59. Mohsen Kadivar, *Andisheh-e Siyasi dar Islam* [Political Thought in Islam], vols. 1–2 (Tehran: Nay Publications, 1998).

60. *Iran Times*, August 24, 2001.

61. Ziba Mir-Hosseini, *Islam and Gender: The Religious Debate in Contemporary Iran* (Princeton: Princeton University Press, 1999).

62. Afshin Molavi, "Read all about it: Iran's newspapers go to war," *Guardian Weekly*, September 19, 1999.

63. Akbar Ganji, *Tarikh-e Khaneh-e Ashbah* [Ghosts' Darkness] (Tehran: Tareh-e Now Publications, 1998), 134.

64. "Who Is Khatami," *Iran Times*, May 30, 1997.

65. "President Khatami Addresses Students," *Iranian National Radio Agency*, December 23, 2001.

66. Cited in *Iran Times*, October 30, 1998.

67. "Children of the Revolution," *Economist*, January 18, 1997.

68. Assad Hedari, "Groupings in the Islamic Republic," *Iran Times*, June 10, 1997.

69. Douglas Jehl, "Iranians Warily Await Reforms They Voted For," *New York Times*, October 10, 1997.

70. Thomas Friedman, "Ayatollah Deng," *New York Times*, July 20, 1999.

71. *Economist*, February 9, 2000.

72. *Economist*, January 16, 2003.

73. "Reformers Allowed on Ballot," *Iran Times*, February 26, 1999.

74. Ayatollah Muhammad Yazdi, *Iran Times*, May 25, 2001.

75. State Department, *Iran: Country Reports on Human Rights Practices* (Washington, DC, 2002), 14.

76. "Khatami Rouses Reform Faithful," *Iran Times*, May 26, 2000.

77. William Samii, "Iran Report," *Radio Free Europe*, June 11, 2001.

78. BBC, August 22, 2002.

79. Ayatollah Mohammad Yazdi, "Freedom of Expression Is Limited," *Iran Times*, April 2, 1999.

80. National Institute for Research Studies, Public Opinion Survey, Radio Free Europe, October 7, 2002.

81. "Lash Rash Breaks Out All over Capital," *Iran Times*, July 20, 2001.

82. "Iran Group Reaffirms Rushdie Death Edict," *New York Times*, February 14, 1998.

83. Abdollah Nouri, *Shokaran-e Aslah* [Hemlock for a Reformer] (Tehran: Tareh-e Now Publications, 1999).

84. John Burns, "Clerics Trail Becomes Flash Point of Iran's Political Fate," *New York Times*, October 31, 1999.

85. Ibrahaim Nabavi, *E'teraf* [Confession] (Tehran: Nay Publication, 2000).

86. *Economist*, January 16, 2003.

87. Majles Deputies, "Open Letter to the Leader," May 24, 2003. www.gooyanews.org.

88. Ian Black, "Europe rebuffs US and Israel to seek trade pact with Iran," *Guardian Weekly*, June 20, 2003.

89. International Monetary Fund, *Staff Report on Iran* (Washington, DC: International Monetary Fund, 2003).

90. Janet Larsen, "Iran's Birth Rate Plummeting at Record Rate," www.thehumanist.org.

91. *Economist*, January 16, 2003.

92. Paul-Marie de La Gorce, "United States Fears a Nuclear Iran," *Le Monde Diplomatique*, December 2002.

93. John Cooley, "More Fingers on Nuclear Trigger?" *Christian Science Monitor*, June 25, 1974.

94. David Sanger, "Weapons Programs," *New York Times*, December 16, 2002.

95. International Institute for Strategic Studies, "Iran's Nuclear Ambitions," *Strategic Comments* 9, no. 2 (April 2003).

96. John Tagliabue, "Summit Leaders Talk Tough on Spread of Nuclear Arms," *New York Times*, June 3, 2003.

97. "Primary Points from the Statement by the Group of 8," *New York Times*, June 3, 2003.

98. Judy Dempsey, "EU warns Iran it may review relations," *Financial Times*, July 22, 2003.

99. Jonathan Steele, "Tehran faces pressure to allow nuclear inspections," *Guardian Weekly*, June 19, 2003.

100. Editorial, *Guardian Weekly*, June 26, 2003.

101. "Iran's fears are real," editorial, *Guardian*, September 16, 2003.

102. Elaine Sciolino, "Nuclear Ambitions Aren't New for Iran," *New York Times*, June 22, 2003.

103. Tagliabue, "Summit Leaders Talk Tough on Spread of Nuclear Arms."

104. Roula Khalaf, "Cleric calls on Iran to defy calls for N-probe," *Financial Times*, September 21, 2003.

105. Hojjatalislam Ali Khamenei, *Ettela'at*, March 5, 1981.

106. Whit Mason, "Iran's Simmering Discontent," *World Policy Journal* XIX, no. 1 (Spring 2002).

107. Neil MacFarquhar, "Millions in Iran Rally Against U.S.," *New York Times*, February 12, 2002.

108. Jahangir Amuzegar, "Iran's Crumbling Revolution," *Foreign Affairs* 82, no. 1 (January 2003), 50.

109. Glenn Kessler, "US signals tough line," *Guardian Weekly*, May 29, 2003.

110. Warren Nelson, "CIA Expecting Islamic Rep. to Evolve, Not Fall," *Iran Times*, November 1, 2002.

111. Steven Weisman, "U.S. Takes Softer Tone on Iran," *New York Times*, October 28, 2003.

112. David Isenberg, "US considers its case on Iran," *Asia Times*, October 31, 2003.

113. Neil MacFarquhar, "Young Iranians are Chafing," *New York Times*, June 16, 2003.

114. Elizabeth Rubin, "The Millimeter Revolution," *New York Times*, April 6, 2003.

115. Jon Sawyer, "Iran: Ripe for Change," *St. Louis Post-Dispatch*, June 15, 2003.

116. International Crisis Group, "Iran: Discontent and Disarray," www.ciriswev.org.

117. Amir Taheri, "Why the Mullahs Fear Her," *New York Post*, October 16, 2003.

118. Geoffrey Kemp, "How to Stop the Iranian Bomb," *National Interest*, Summer 2003.

119. Gary Sick cited in Mark Follman, "Is Iran Next?," www.salon.com/news/feature/2003/nuclear_iran.

120. Robert Malley and John Morris, "Iran: Don't Count on a New Revolution," *Los Angeles Times*, August 11, 2003.

3

DAMASCUS VS. WASHINGTON: BETWEEN THE "AXIS OF EVIL" AND "PAX AMERICANA"

Moshe Ma'oz

"FOR THREE TRANSGRESSIONS OF DAMASCUS AND FOR FOUR . . . " AMOS 1:3

In the wake of the American-Iraqi war of 2003, American-Syrian relations are on a collision course. As a symptom of this tension, a vitriolic war of words has developed. Bushra Kanafani, the spokeswoman of the Syrian foreign ministry articulated it last October rather diplomatically, "Syrian-American relations have deteriorated markedly in recent years." Her superior, Foreign Minister Faruq Al-Shar'a, sounded less diplomatic when in July 2003 he described the Bush administration as being, "the most violent and stupidest." American diplomats and other officials were more blunt. Ari Fleischer, the White House spokesman, called Syria a "rogue nation," while another administration official said that Syria is "behaving badly" and that along with Libya and Cuba, Syria was regarded as "junior varsity axis of evil." Other officials and analysts have gone even further, stressing that Ba'thist Syria is "qualified" to replace Ba'thist Iraq in President Bush's original "axis of evil" alongside Iran and North Korea. Stating that "there's got to be a change in Syria," some Americans have even suggested that Syria should therefore become the next target of U.S. attack and conquest,[1] aiming at toppling the Bashar Ba'th regime and establishing a new democratic system in Damascus.

Many more Americans — including most members of Congress — have advocated imposing severe economic and diplomatic sanctions on Damascus to punish it for perceived transgressions. In American eyes, these transgressions include three in particular that have been related to the American war against Iraq and four others that have been committed over a longer period of recent history, namely:

1. *Syria's vociferous opposition to the U.S. war against Iraq.*
   Syrian President Bashar Asad expressed the wish that the United States would either be defeated militarily or be forced to flee by internal resistance. He stated inter alia: "this time some Arab capitals will stand beside Baghdad . . . it does not . . . exclude Syria, which is the closest and at the heart of battles against invaders, because [Damascus] is the heart of Arabism. . . . They [America] removed their masks and said they wanted oil and that they wanted to redraw the map of the region in accordance with Israeli interests. [This war] will serve Israel through its control of the American administration."[2]

2. *Syria's harboring of Iraqi fugitives, weapons, and assets.*
   Syria is alleged to have taken in Iraqi regime fugitives — and also allegedly Iraqi weapons of mass destruction — to hide them from coalition forces; along with accepting $3 billion in Saddam's assets by government-controlled Syrian banks, while buying billions of dollars worth of cheap Iraqi oil in violation of UN sanctions on Iraq.[3]

3. *Syria's aiding of Iraq by opening its border to military smuggling.*
   Syria is alleged to have encouraged armed volunteer fighters — mostly Syrian — to cross the Iraqi border to participate in anti-American guerrilla actions and to have also facilitated the flow of military equipment into Iraq.

Four longer-term Syrian transgressions in American eyes have been:

1. *Development of weapons of mass destruction.*

   Syrian chemical weapons capabilities, developed since the 1970s are highly advanced. Damascus has a stockpile of the nerve agent Sarin that can be delivered by aircraft or ballistic missile and has developed the more toxic VX nerve agent. Additionally, with North Korean and Iranian help, Syria has developed and acquired long-range SCUD missiles that can reach much of Israel along with portions of Turkey, Iraq, and Jordan.[4] At the same time Syria is continuing to develop the "poor man's nuclear weapon," namely biological weapons capabilities, that are extremely lethal. With Russian assistance, Syria has started a civic nuclear power program that could facilitate a nuclear weapons capability.

2. *Ongoing Syrian state sponsorship of terrorism.*

   Syria has been accused of harboring and backing some ten terrorist and guerrilla organizations, mostly Islamic ones, notably the Lebanese Hezbollah, Palestinian Hamas, and Islamic Jihad. Damascus has allegedly provided these groups with training facilities (and with Iranian cooperation), weapons, and funding. These militant organizations continue to operate in Syria despite American warnings.

3. *Continued domination of Lebanon.*

   Syria has had more than 25,000 troops, mostly in the strategically important Bekáa Valley, in Lebanon since the mid-1970s, and continues to support the Hezbollah militia in coordination with its close ally Iran. Syria continues to indirectly control the Lebanese government and dictate policy.

4. *Maintaining an authoritarian and anti-democratic regime.*

   Some Americans accuse Syria's Ba'thist regime of continuing to brutally suppress the human rights and freedoms of speech and assembly of its own citizens and labels Syria as a police state, well known for prohibiting free expression, jailing and torturing members of the opposition, and allowing only political parties that support the Ba'thist regime. Syrian election results are organized and known in advance.

Vis-à-vis these Syrian transgressions, in September 2002 the U.S. House of Representatives Committee on International Relations began its hearings on the Syrian Accountability Act (SAA). Through the SAA, the House committee has sought to impose economic and diplomatic sanctions against Syria for its continued occupation of Lebanon, support of terrorist organizations, development of ballistic missiles, and illegal importation of Iraqi oil.[5] The Bush administration initially distanced itself from this act (for almost a year), asking the committee members not to move forward on this bill, lest it would limit the U.S. options with regard to Syria. But as of October 2003, the White House dropped its opposition to the sanctions bill, due to Syrian behavior, particularly on the issue of terrorism, and in the context of America's officially proclaimed War on Terrorism.

On October 15, 2003, the U.S. House of Representatives voted 398 to 4 to impose economic and diplomatic sanctions on Syria, unless it ceases to support terrorist groups and withdraws its troops from Lebanon. Among the penalties that can be imposed by the U.S. president on Syria are a freeze on Syrian assets in the United States, a halt in American business investment in Syria, a ban on U.S. exports to Syria, a reduction in diplomatic contacts, restrictions on Syrian diplomats, and a prohibition on the use of U.S. airports by Syrian aircraft.

Yet even before this sanctions bill was approved, Washington adopted some strong measures against Syria, in addition to voicing stern threats against Damascus. The Iraqi-Syrian oil pipeline was disconnected by Americans in Iraq, thus depriving Damascus of cheap Iraqi oil, and on June 18, 2003, U.S. military forces penetrated from Iraq into Syria in pursuit of a convoy allegedly carrying fugitive Iraqi leaders. Many Syrian soldiers were killed during this incursion and five Syrian border guards were taken into custody by U.S. troops.

Perhaps even more crucial was President Bush's approval of

Israel's airstrike on an alleged Palestinian terrorist training base near Damascus. This strike, the first since 1973, was in retaliation for a suicide bombing by a female member of the Islamic Jihad in Haifa, Israel, on October 4, 2003, that killed twenty Israelis, Jews and Arabs alike. President Bush reacted to the Israeli raid as follows: "Israel's got the right to defend itself. Israel must not feel constrained in defending its homeland."[6]

It would thus appear that Washington's strategy toward Damascus since the Iraq war has been as stated in the biblical passage of Amos 1:3, "For three transgressions of Damascus and for four I will not revoke its punishment." In modern terminology this would probably mean that Syria has become a full member in Bush's doctrine of the "axis of evil," alongside Iran and North Korea, and is subject to U.S. economic and diplomatic sanctions.

The intriguing and crucial questions are:

1. Would Washington also employ military pressures against Damascus, perhaps even attack Syria (which is militarily much easier than attacking Iran or North Korea), or will President Bush simply tolerate it if Israeli prime minister Ariel Sharon continues attacking Syria after each suicide bombing by a militant Palestinian?
2. What can be the repercussions of Israeli or American military action against Syria?
3. Should Washington adopt a totally different strategy toward Damascus—i.e., being positive rather than negative, cooperative rather than rejectionist. Or in other words, employ political and diplomatic means as well as economic carrots to integrate Syria into a new U.S. strategic regional network—a constructive brand of Pax Americana?

In order to implement an alternative regional policy such as may be suggested by the last question above, a peace agreement between Syria and Israel is assumed in cooperation with other pro-American regimes in the region such as Turkey, Jordan,

Egypt, Saudi Arabia, and a new Iraq. Such a strategic network can render stability to the region, effectively combating Islamic militant terrorism while inducing Syria to cease its domination over Lebanon, reform its political system and economic infrastructure, and improve its poor record in the area of human rights.

It would indeed appear that Syrian president Bashar Asad has been inclined since his ascendancy to reform his country's economic and political systems and mitigate his harsh measures in the area of human rights. He has also pursued his father's legacy of seeking peace with Israel in return for the Golan Heights.

Finally, Asad and other Syrian officials have voiced conciliatory statements toward Washington since the end of the Iraqi war, while Damascus has also cooperated with the CIA in hunting down al-Qaida terrorists, and thus "saved American lives."[7] On October 16, 2003, as a member of the UN Security Council, Syria voted in favor of the U.S.-UK resolution authorizing an American-led multinational force in Iraq.

What can these Syrian actions and gestures imply with regard to future relations between Damascus and Washington? What are the Syrian and American options concerning each other?

The aims of the remainder of this chapter are to carefully examine the potential Syrian strategies, while drawing upon the record of the Ba'th regime, notably since the ascendancy of Hafiz Asad in 1970. It will survey and analyze the development of Syrian policies in the international, regional, and domestic arenas, addressing major issues such as the U.S.-USSR conflict, the Arab-Israeli dispute, the Iraq-Iran and Iraq-Kuwait wars, and the Lebanese civil war, as well as the problems of terrorism and political rights.

This chapter will explore the calculations, motivations, ideologies, interests, constraints, and advantages that formulated the positions or strategies of Syria, and what lessons Washington can draw regarding future relations with Damascus.

THE SETTING

Like other Arab states in the Middle East, modern Syria was carved out of the collapsing Ottoman-Turkish Empire after World War I through the previously signed Sykes-Picot Agreement (1916) divided the region between Great Britain and France.

Although allocated to France by this agreement, Syria became in 1918, with British backing, a semi-independent Arab emirate under Emir Faysal, who later became King Faysal I as Syria evolved into a Syrian-Arab kingdom. A former commander-in-chief of the Arab revolt against the Ottoman Turks (1916–17), Faysal sought further British support to continue his rule in Damascus, contrary to French designs for Syria (and Lebanon). However, despite its previous vague promise to grant parts of Syria to Arabs, Great Britain did not prevent France from ousting Faysal by force in 1920 and establishing a mandated regime in Syria and Lebanon.

The League of Nations approved the French Mandate, but most Syrian-Arabs resented it, preferring independence, or at least temporary American supervision, leading to an independent state.

Lasting until World War II, the French Mandate did very little to practically prepare Syria for independence, except that it indirectly contributed to a consolidation of Syrian-Arab nationalism. This was characterized by intense, anti-French, anti-Western antagonism. Great Britain helped the Syrians to gain independence from the French Vichy (pro-Nazi) rule during World War II (1941), leading to the formal establishment of a Syrian-Arab republic in 1946. However, London subsequently alienated

Syrian nationalists by its continued military presence and influence in the region (particularly in Iraq, Jordan, and Egypt). This long-term, regional influence was evidenced in 1955 by Britain's creation of the Baghdad Pact with the pro-Western states of Iraq, Turkey, Iran, and Pakistan. Although directed against the Soviet Union, this pact was considered by Damascus as a strategic threat to itself, particularly from Turkey and Iraq, in addition to the existing tension with pro-American Israel (which was not a signatory of the Baghdad Pact).

In late 1954, Syria had already reacted to a perceived Western threat by becoming the first Arab state to seek military assistance from the Soviet Bloc by signing a small arms deal with Czechoslovakia. It is true that two Syrian rulers, Husni Za'im and Adib Shishakli, during the years of 1949–54 developed close relations with the United States, notably with the CIA, but by and large, Syrian politicians and officials expressed growing antagonism toward Washington, owing to President Truman's support for the creation of the State of Israel in 1948, its backing of the Baghdad Pact, and the proclamation in 1957 of the Eisenhower doctrine. This doctrine aimed at strengthening pro-Western Arab regimes and combating the expansion of Communism (i.e., Soviet influence) in the region, notably in Syria and Egypt. It is interesting to note at this juncture the arguments that Eisenhower's secretary of state, John Foster Dulles, made in an attempt to persuade the Syrians that the Soviets are their enemies, not their allies.

In a circular to American embassies in the Middle East, Dulles suggested:

> . . . present Soviet support Arab states as purely tactical . . . point out that Soviet Bloc supported establishment Israel and partition Palestine furnished arms to Israel during Palestine War . . . pro-Soviet regime in Syria does not have support of Syrian people, op-

position to present Syrian regime is led by "free" Arab
countries that see their hard-won independence and
their security threatened by traitor to nationalist
cause, betraying Arabs to new foreign [Soviet] imperialism; "free" Arab countries do not compromise
their position with respect to Israel by cooperation
with Free world.[8]

Yet the U.S. State Department was not content with mere
guidelines. Since early 1956 it had entertained plans to topple the
Syrian, pro-Soviet regime and reinstate Col. Adib Shishakli, a
pro-American leader who had originally seized power in December 1949 and established a brutal dictatorship that lasted until
February 1954, when he was ousted by a military coup. Thus, on
June 27, 1956, the American assistant secretary of state wrote a
memo to Secretary Dulles with the following conclusions:

Adib Shishakli falls clearly short of the type of a leader
we should like Syria to have, but he might be better
than some other potential candidates . . . consequently we should bide our time and await develop-
ments before taking any positive position relative to
his possible return to power.[9]

The Syrian authorities apparently detected such American intentions and also suspected American subversive activities; all of
which enhanced Damascus's animosity and alienation toward
Washington. Thus, according to official Syrian sources, Washington masterminded a plot in August 1957, to overthrow the
Syrian government and replace it with a pro-Western regime.[10]
This plot was allegedly coordinated with Turkey, Iraq, Jordan,
and Israel as well. Turkey had massed troops along its southern
border with Syria, while Israel had been engaged for years in
mutual hostilities along its ceasefire line with Syria.

Besieged and vulnerable, the Syrian government, influenced by the leftist-radical Ba'th and Communist parties, strengthened its military and diplomatic ties with the USSR; and induced by the Pan-Arab Ba'thist politicians and army officers, Syria intensified its political and military ties with Egypt, then ruled by the Pan-Arab leader Gamal 'Abd al-Nasir (transliterated as Nasser). In October 1956, Damascus and Cairo signed a military pact, and in February 1958, these two states merged in an unprecedented union: the United Arab Republic (UAR) under the supreme leadership of Nasser. However, this union was not one of equals. Because the Syrian regime was infused with a high degree of paranoia, vis-à-vis external threats, it was desperate and agreed to the union without any preconditions in the hope of gaining Egyptian protection against its enemies. Additionally, Nasser was the preeminent regional leader at the time, and took advantage of this opportunity to dominate Syria.

A few months later in July 1958, pro-Nasserist officers staged a bloody coup in Iraq, toppling the pro-Western Hashemite monarchy and establishing a radical revolutionary regime headed by General Qasim. These two major upheavals contributed to destabilizing two more pro-Western Arab regimes in the region: the Hashemite Kingdom of Jordan and the Christian Maronite–led Lebanese government. At the request of these governments, thousands of American marines were deployed in Lebanon, along with British paratroopers in Jordan, in order to fend off any chance of Pan-Arab coups.

Washington however, rejected Israel's request to obtain American arms or to be included in a new American-sponsored regional alliance, vis-à-vis a Soviet-backed UAR. A major reason for this American rejection was to avoid alienating the UAR while trying to contain it as a potential regional menace.

Therefore, a U.S. National Security Council policy paper of November 1958 suggested inter alia the following guidelines:

> Endeavor to establish effective working relations with
> Arab nationalism while at the same time seeking con-
> structively to influence and stabilize the movement and
> to contain its outward thrust, and recognizing that a
> policy of U.S. accommodation to . . . radical Pan-Arab
> nationalism as symbolized by Nasser would include
> many elements contrary to U.S. interests. . . . While
> seeking pro-Western orientation, accept neutralist pol-
> icies of states in the area when necessary. . . . Continue
> limitation on shipments of arms to Israel . . . solicit the
> assistance of other nations in implementing this policy
> of limitation.[11]

To be sure, the United States failed to gain the goodwill and
cooperation of the UAR, nor was it successful in weakening Nasser's strategic relations with the USSR. The Soviets not only became the major supplier of weapons to the UAR, but assumed
also a major role in its foreign policy as well as in its economic
development.

Already in 1958, Moscow undertook to help construct Egypt's
Aswan High Dam, following the withdrawal of U.S. financial
assistance for this huge project in 1956. However, despite the massive Soviet help, and the popular support among Arab nationalists, the Egyptian-Syrian union was far from becoming a success
story for Pan-Arabism. Rather, this union turned out to be an
Egyptian domination of Syria in the political, military, and economic arenas. Syrian political leaders were removed from senior
positions, all Syrian political parties, including the Ba'th, were
dissolved and many military officers were forced to resign or be
relocated to Egypt, while the upper class of Syrian landowners
and businessmen were severely hit by Nasser's socialist reforms.
Syria was being ruled by a heavy hand from Cairo, with Egyptian
intelligence officers in control.

Consequently, anti-Egyptian resentment developed, Pan-Arab solidarity decreased, and in September 1961 Syrian military officers staged a coup leading to Syria's secession from the UAR. Military officers continued to crucially impact on the civilian, conservative Syrian governments that were formed after the 1961 coup. In March 1963, younger and more radical military officers initiated another coup, which led to the establishment of the Ba'th regime in Damascus; a regime that still controls the Syrian Arab Republic to this day.

SYRIAN POLITICS: THE MILITARY, THE BA'TH, AND ALAWITES

Upon gaining its formal independence from the French mandatory rule in 1946, Syria became a republic and established a parliamentary democratic system, partly derived from the French era. Yet, this system did not authentically and equally represent all sections of the population. It was in effect run by members of the upper and upper-middle classes—composed of landowners, merchants, and tribal chiefs. Mostly Sunni Muslims, they held most of the land, the big businesses and dominated the political parties.

Among those, the two major, veteran, nationalist parties that intermittently controlled the government and the parliament were the Nationalist Party based predominantly in Damascus, the capital, and the People's Party, centered in Aleppo (the other large city in Syria). Vis-à-vis these nationalist conservative parties, three small, radical, and more modern parties claimed to represent the lower classes of the society, peasants and workers. But their main activists were young intellectuals and army officers, and many of them were members of the non-Sunni heterodox sects and non-Muslim minorities such as Christians, Alawites, Druze, Isma'ilis, along with Sunni Kurds, who were not Arab.

The first of these small and ideological parties was the Communist Party, which had started operating in Lebanon in the mid-1920s and in Syria in the 1930s. Led by its charismatic secretary-general, Khalid Baqdash, a Kurd from Damascus, the tiny Communist Party was obviously pro-Soviet, anti-West, but supported Arab nationalism. The French and Syrian authorities periodically persecuted it, but in the free democratic elections of 1954, Baqdash was elected to the parliament and became the first Communist delegate to serve in any Arab parliament. The Communist influence which affected Syrian politics reached beyond the parliament into other segments of Syrian society and spread among professionals, intellectuals, "front organizations," and army officers. The Communists became particularly influential during the mid-1950s when Syria developed close ties with the Soviet Union; and in 1957 one of the pro-Communist military officers, Afif Bizri, was appointed as chief of staff of the Syrian army, holding this position until the creation of the Syrian-Egyptian union.

Another small ideological party, which initially competed, with the Ba'th party was the Syrian Nationalist Party (Parti Populaire Syrienne or PPS), later renamed the Syrian Social Nationalist Party (SSNP), and founded in Beirut in the early 1930s by the charismatic Anton Sa'adah, a Greek Orthodox Christian. This party reflected unique ideology and organization. It professed non-Arab, Syrian nationalism, embracing the people of "Greater Syria," which included people living also in Lebanon, Palestine, Jordan, and sometimes, Iraq and Cyprus. Organized in a military-fascist manner (under the influence of fascist Germany and Italy), the party plotted in 1949 to topple the Lebanese government, in order to incorporate Lebanon into Syria. But, its leader Sa'adah was extradited by Syria to Lebanon, where he was promptly executed.

Members and followers of the party continued their activities in Lebanon, mostly operating underground, owing to Lebanese government harassment. In Syria itself, however, this party after securing two seats in the 1954 parliamentary elections, gained significant influence among young army officers. They struggled against their Ba'thist rivals resorting also to the assassination of a senior Ba'th officer, the army's deputy commander in chief. In reaction, the PPS was outlawed while its members were harshly persecuted in the army and beyond, although some of the party's Pan-Syrian ideas left their imprint on various Syrian quarters, notably the Ba'thist leadership. Unlike the Syrian Social Nationalist Party (which later also adopted Arabism) and the Communists that have since remained marginal in Syrian politics, the Ba'th Party managed through its military supporters to seize power in Damascus on March 8, 1963, and has continued its rule for the last forty years.

In Iraq the Ba'th party seized power briefly in February 1963 and then from July 1968 to April 2003. Branches of the Ba'th Party have also operated in Lebanon, Jordan, and in the Palestinian territories. Yet Damascus was the birthplace of the Ba'th (renaissance) Party which was founded in the mid-1940s by two noncharismatic high school teachers: Michel Aflaq, a Greek Orthodox Christian Arab and the party's ideologist, and Salah ad-Din al-Bitar, a Sunni Muslim and the party's secretary. They were soon joined by Zaki Arsuzi, an intellectual who came from the Muslim heterodox Alawite sect (12 percent of the population). Initially the party represented mainly young, urban intellectuals and members of rural minority groups. In late 1953 the Ba'th Party merged with Akram Hawrani's Arab Socialist Party (predominantly consisting of Sunni Muslim peasants).

It was renamed the Ba'th Arab Socialist Party, and unlike its small rival parties, it professed Pan-Arab unity, non-Marxist socialism, along with freedom of speech and association, as well as liberation from imperialism, colonialism, and socioreligious sectarianism.

Although it was secular in its approach, the Ba'th Party acknowledged the Islamic cultural-historical roots of Arabism. Nevertheless, it did not appeal to conservative Sunni Muslim sections of the population because of its secular tendencies, its socialist platform, as well as its largely non-Sunni membership. Conservative Sunni Muslims were more attracted to the Muslim Brotherhood movement, which was established in the late 1930s on the model of the original movement founded in Egypt some ten years earlier. But the Syrian Muslim Brothers led by Mustafa al-Sibai' (from 1945 to 1961) were not as popular as the Ba'th Party; in the 1954 democratic elections they gained only 5 seats in the parliament, compared to the 22 seats scored by the Ba'th Party, out of 142 parliament seats total.

Obviously with such a relatively small membership, the Ba'th Party could not control the parliament or the government in which they took part. In fact, the Ba'th derived its main influence from the allegiance of the Syrian military officer corps, who since 1949 had intervened in national politics and assumed a powerful position both through military coups as well as behind the scenes.

The first military coup occurred in March 1949, following the poor performance of the Syrian army in the 1948 all-Arab war against the newly born State of Israel. Col. Husni Za'im (partly Kurdish) who led the coup with CIA backing, blamed the civilian government of neglecting to allocate sufficient resources for the war effort.

He also criticized the government for its immobility in domestic affairs, failures in foreign policies, and mismanagement and corruption of the parliamentary system. Za'im established a tough military dictatorship, dissolved all political parties, and introduced social-secular reforms. He was himself toppled in August 1949 by a counter military coup led by Col. Sami Hinnawi, who officially returned the reins of power to a civilian government led by the People's Party. But in December 1949 a third military coup brought to power Col. Adib Shishakli, who remained in charge for more than four years, laying some groundwork for molding Syria as a nation-state, while reforming its society and improving its economy.

For the first two years, Shishakli controlled Syria behind the scenes as deputy chief of staff of the army, allowing civilian politicians to form the government. But owing to disagreements with this government, a growing conflict between the dominant People's Party and the rival Nationalist Party, Shishakli dissolved both the government and parliament in late 1951. He then established a brutal military dictatorship, especially oppressing democratic groups and the Muslim Brothers as well as the rebellious Druze community (4 percent of the population).

In his foreign policy, Shishakli, like Za'im, was not keen to unify Syria with other Arab states or to rely on the USSR; rather he developed close ties with the United States and was prepared to join a Western alliance vis-à-vis the Soviet Union. With American inducements he also offered to conclude a peace treaty (in fact a nonbelligerency agreement) with Israel, and absorb half a million Palestinian refugees; provided he would get American financial support of $200 million and have Israel concede to Syria part of Lake Tiberias.

Shishakli was ousted in February 1954 not essentially owing to his pragmatic attitudes toward the United States and Israel, but due to his harsh regime and measures that alienated most sections of the population—conservative and radical alike. Representatives and followers of these sections in the military officer corps, backed by the outlawed political parties and many students, coordinated and launched a military coup under the command of a lieutenant colonel and a few majors. Although a civilian parliamentary regime was subsequently reinstated in Syria and free democratic elections were conducted, the military officer corps continued to be a major focus of power.

As it happened, many army officers were associated with the small radical parties—the Ba'th, the Communists, and the PPS; since nationalist and/or socialist ideas and the 1948 Arab-Israeli War had radicalized them. Some of these officers, notably the Ba'thists, advanced in their ranks and positions rather quickly, owing on the one hand to the special connections of Ba'thist leaders (especially Hawrani's) with the army command, on the other hand because many veteran officers were purged or forced to retire after the four military coups that had occurred since 1949.

A significant number of those young Ba'thist officers were members of minority groups, especially Alawite and Druze. This phenomenon was in line with the preceding trend of young and poor Alawites and Druze to join the "Special Troops" during the mandatory period; the French would utilize their combative tradition and train them to put down Syrian nationalist uprisings or disturbances; and these young Alawites and Druze would use their military careers for socioeconomic mobility. This trend continued after Syrian independence and was also characterized by the tendency of Druze and Alawites (and also young Sunnis from small towns and villages) to serve in combat units, including commando units.

Their proportion in those units was rather high, much higher than their proportion in the whole population. During the 1950s many of these soldiers were promoted to higher ranks or positions thanks to their experience and Ba'thist contacts. It is therefore not surprising that among the thirteen-member "military committee" that contrived the 1963 Ba'thist coup three were Alawites, two were Druze. Two of these Alawite officers—Col. Salah Jadid and Capt. Hafiz Asad—later became rulers of Ba'thist Syria.

THE BA'TH AND NEO-BA'TH REGIMES:
THE SUNNI-ALAWITE RIFT

Military officers—Alawite, Druze, and mostly Sunnis (members of the majority population)—held the reins of power in Damascus following the March 1963 coup. The veteran civilian Ba'th leaders and founders—notably Aflaq and Bitar—were marginalized and later left Syria. Aflaq joined the rival Ba'th regime in Baghdad, while Bitar went to France and, in 1980, more than a decade after leaving Syria, was assassinated in Paris, probably by Hafiz Asad's agents because of criticism of Asad's regime. In addition, the policies of the military-led Ba'th regime also significantly deviated from the original Ba'th Party notions of Arab unity, non-Marxist Socialism, and freedom. The new Ba'thist rulers, although hailing Pan-Arabism and Arab unity, tended in practice to mold Syria as an independent nation-state. They did participate in the futile Arab unity talks with Egypt and Iraq in March-April 1963, but subsequently they developed intense conflicts with these two radical Arab regimes.

The new rulers of Syria, representing the lower and rural sections of the population, diverted also from the original moderate-socialist Ba'thist thinking. They carried out a strict Marxist-Socialist policy—confiscating large quantities of land from large- and medium-size landowners and distributing parts of the land to landless peasants; nationalizing industrial and commercial firms and transferring their management to state and party officials. The Ba'th regime also interpreted differently the original Ba'th Party's ideas regarding political freedom and the role of Islam in society. They imposed a one-party autocratic system, as well as strict secular measures—brutally suppressing both liberal and Islamic opposition groups.

But as it happened, within the Ba'th regime intense conflicts developed between party and army militants and pragmatists,

Sunnis and Alawites, as well as between top leaders. Although there was not always a precise correlation between these conflicts, positions and alliances did shift, and personal and factional sectarian factors remained dominant. Thus for example, Syria's strongman during the years 1963–66, Gen. Amin al-Hafiz, a Sunni Muslim, was challenged by the Alawite general Salah Jadid who as the new chief of staff of the Syrian army, appointed Alawite officers to key military positions as well as enlisted many more young Alawites to the officer corps. Together with his Alawite comrade Hafiz Asad, the air force commander, Jadid concluded alliances with Druze and other non-Sunni officers.

On February 23, 1966, Jadid and his allies seized power in Damascus, by means of a bloody coup, attempting to justify their brutal action by ideological arguments. While establishing a radical Marxist government—the so-called neo-Ba'th rule—and becoming now the Ba'th Party boss, Jadid disposed of his ambitious Druze allies and appointed party activists to senior government offices.

However, he was subsequently challenged by his fellow Alawite, Hafiz Asad, who also assumed the position of defense minister and mobilized the support of key military units, dismissing Jadid's accomplices. This personal rivalry between the two Syrian-Alawite leaders reflected the party-army struggle for power, as well as the two diverse approaches regarding Syria's domestic, regional, and global policies. Asad opposed the dogmatic Marxist, socialist, and secular measures of Jadid that alienated many Syrians, particularly large sections of the Sunni Muslim majority population.

He suggested relaxing these measures and assuming more moderate pragmatic socioeconomic policies, while also allocating a larger part of the budget to expand the armed forces, even at the expense of economic development. This demand was made not merely to please the military establishment and win their allegiance; Asad's major concern at that juncture and later, was Syria's military and strategic inferiority vis-à-vis Israel.

This grave imbalance was demonstrated during the June 1967 war, when Israel easily defeated the Syrian, Egyptian, and Jordanian armies and in only six days of combat, occupied the Syrian Golan (Jawlan), the Egyptian Sinai and Gaza, and the Jordanian-held West Bank area.

Furthermore, in Asad's view, Syria's security and its strategic balance with Israel was also linked to Damascus's relations with neighboring Arab states regardless of their political-ideological orientations. He rejected Jadid's antagonism toward conservative Arab regimes, notably Jordan, as well as toward the newly established (July 1968) Ba'th regime in Iraq. Asad also disagreed with Jadid's support of a "popular liberation war" by Palestinian guerrilla organizations instead of a regular military confrontation vis-à-vis Israel. In his address to a Ba'th convention in March 1969 Asad stated:

> I have repeatedly stressed the importance of Arab military coordination, notably among the Arab states, which border with Israel, regardless of the differences and the contradictions in their political positions, as long as it would serve the armed struggle . . . the defensive capability of the Syrian front is closely tied with the capability of other Arab fronts . . . the same mistake prior to June 5 [1967] could be repeated and Israel would be able to strike at each of the Arab fronts separately, one after the other. Therefore, the escalation and the continuation of the [Palestinian] *fida'yi* [guerrilla] action is largely tied up with the defensive capability of the Arab fronts.[12]

No wonder then that Asad's motive, pretext, or timing for deposing Jadid was linked to Syrian regional policies, notably its conflict with Israel. In September 1970, Jadid dispatched Syrian tank units to Jordan to help the Palestinian guerrillas in their uprising against King Hussein's regime. As commander of the Syrian Air Force, Asad denied air cover for these units since he was concerned about an Israeli military intervention with an American "green light"—it was likely to destroy Syria's fighter planes as well as its tanks. It is also possible that Asad did not wish to alienate King Hussein, the leader of a strategically important "confrontation" state with Israel, by backing a Palestinian rebellion, which was likely to fail in the event of American-Israeli military intervention.[13]

Finally, two more crucial events possibly contributed to Asad's decision to seize power in Damascus. Egypt's president Nasser died on September 28, 1970, thus potentially increasing Syria's vulnerability vis-à-vis Israel. Nasser's successor, Anwar Sadat, invited Sudan, Libya, and Syria to form a federal union with Egypt. Jadid turned down this offer, while Asad considered such a union essential to Syria's strategic balance with Israel. Asad wasted no time in adopting rigid measures against Jadid's political and military supporters and on November 16, 1970, he completed his military coup by arresting Jadid and his Ba'thist comrades.

On March 12, 1971, Asad was elected as Syria's president by a popular referendum with 99.2 percent of the vote. A new phase began in the annals of Syrian history and politics, lasting for thirty years, an unprecedented period in modern Syrian history.

HAFIZ ASAD: A BALANCE SHEET

Asad established for the first time in modern Syrian history a powerful, centralized, presidential regime, rendering Syria unprecedented domestic stability and regional influence. His auto-cratic rule derived from several sources:

1. The extensive formal powers granted to him by the new constitution in the political, military, judicial, and economic sectors.
2. The informal apparatus for control and inspection by his close comrades—the Jama'a (the Band) consisted of senior politi-cians and military officers, Sunnis and Alawites alike.
3. The security belt: made up of some ten security and intelli-gence networks as well as special forces, the Republican Guard, and combat military units. Those forces were em-ployed to harshly persecute opposition elements and to bru-tally quell Islamic uprisings.
4. The Ba'th Party: rendering Asad legitimacy and serving as an instrument of mobilization, indoctrination, and supervision of the Syrian population.
5. Asad's unique personality and leadership reflecting strength, authority, consistency, endurance, and strategic thinking. Even American leaders who spent time with him, (Nixon, Carter, and Kissinger) praised his intellectual qualities.

Since his ascendancy, Asad attempted to blur his Alawite military-based autocracy, and presented himself as a legitimate Syrian-Arab-Muslim ruler, deriving his authority directly from the people who would elect him every seven years as president by at least 99 percent of the vote. Yet Asad was the only candidate in these presidential referenda and did not hesitate to remove any potential contenders for power, including his own brother Rifat.

Asad appointed many Sunni Muslims to senior positions in the government and the Ba'th Party, as well as to other public positions, in an attempt to demonstrate that members of the Ala-wite minority did not dominate his regime. But his huge security belt was commanded by Alawites from his and his wife's family, clan, and village, as well as from other loyal Alawite tribes. In addition, select loyal Sunni Muslims, as well as men from different minority groups, were enlisted to these security apparatuses and combat units, including Christians, Druze, Circassians, and Turkmens. In order to exhibit his regime as "pluralist," "popular," and a "democracy," Asad, unlike Jadid, permitted six small parties—including socialist, nationalist, and two communist parties—to function and participate in parliamentary elections.

In 1972, these parties, together with the leading Ba'th Party, formed a "national progressive front" in the parliament, which since 1990 gained two-thirds of the parliamentary seats (out of a total of 250); most of which are held by Ba'th delegates. About half of the seats in the parliament were allocated to peasants and workers, and about one-third to "independent" delegates, namely professionals, businessmen, urban notables, tribal chiefs, Muslim clergy, and women. Parliament members would normally discuss, and also criticize, economic, social, and administrative policies, but absolutely not issues concerning security and foreign affairs, the state budget, human rights, and the presidency.

Still, on various occasions, a few leaders of the Communist Party and of associations of lawyers, doctors, and engineers did publicly blame the government for its brutality against the Muslim opposition and its abuse of civil rights. They demanded the abolition of the state's draconian emergency laws. The authorities managed to neutralize these critics or have them dismissed from their public positions.

Nevertheless, large sections of the population, including Sunni Muslims, apparently supported Asad's regime, and publicly took part in his personality cult. Among those were peasants and workers who were grateful to Asad (as well as to previous Ba'thist governments) for the significant improvement of their standard of living, their socioeconomic mobility, and their health and education services.

Asad partly pursued the socioeconomic change, perhaps a "revolution," that had started on a large scale during the UAR era and continued under Ba'thist rule, namely land reform and nationalization of big industry and commerce. Yet Asad introduced certain important alterations in Syria's economic policies aiming at promoting a private sector in urban and rural areas alike, while also maintaining the public sector. He encouraged private investment and initiatives in industry, commerce, and tourism, as well as in agriculture—permitting again medium-size land ownership, while also expanding state-run agricultural cooperatives. The major results of Asad's new economic policies, starting in the early 1970s and reinforced since the early 1990s included the emergence of a new socioeconomic middle class, consisting of businessmen, industrialists, and entrepreneurs, mostly Sunni Muslims. Many of them developed social ties and business partnerships with senior Alawite officers, thus creating a new Sunni-Alawite alliance that provided a support base for the regime.

By contrast, however, many workers, peasants, and public employees who had formed the backbone of the previous Ba'thist governments were left behind, becoming impoverished. This growing hardship in Syrian society also occurred as a result of the high military expenditure of Asad's regime as well as the poor performance of the public sector.

Apart from the relatively new and profitable oil industry, the public sector continued to be significantly plagued by mismanagement, inefficiency, corruption, nepotism, and over-employment. These chronic problems were compounded by huge demographic growth, due to a high birthrate, and brought about fresh pressures on the government budget and state services.

Consequently, unemployment increased (particularly in the public sector) and wages decreased, while more poor peasants immigrated to towns, expanding the ranks of the embittered urban proletariat. Despite their potential threat to the regime's stability, these restless poor sectors were not organized, were strictly watched by the secret services and police, and could be bought-off by periodic government subsidies.

Other opposition elements were similarly unorganized and closely supervised, including liberal intellectuals and professionals who disagreed with the government's suppression of political freedoms and breaches of human rights, as well as radical-leftist Ba'thists who disapproved of Asad's deviation from the socialist tenets of the first Ba'th regime. The only highly organized and motivated opposition to Asad's regime was the militant wing of the "Muslim Brothers," who posed a serious menace to his rule.

THE ISLAMIC CHALLENGE

Until the ascendancy of the Ba'th officers in 1963, the Muslim Brothers had constituted a nonviolent socioreligious movement. It preached for the enhancement of Syria's Islamic character as well as for Muslim education among the population. This movement participated in the general elections under various "front" organizations or as "independent" delegates—securing in the 1954 elections five seats in the parliament (see also above) and in the 1961 elections, ten seats out of 150 parliament members.

But, upon the establishment of the Ba'th regime in 1963, the Muslim Brothers were outlawed along with all other political parties. Yet, unlike most other parties, the Muslim Brothers could survive and even expand their ranks thanks to their compartmentalized underground network, as well as their powerful indoctrination and education system predicated in thousands of mosques throughout the country. This Islamic movement, representing also grievances of nonreligious Sunni Muslims, resented the new Ba'thist measures of separating Islam from the state, secularizing public life, reducing Islamic (and Christian) teaching in state schools, as well as dismissing hundreds of Muslim clerics and decreasing the jurisdiction and income of many others. In addition more Sunni Muslims were hurt by the Ba'thist's severe socialist measures that appropriated their lands, businesses, factories, and banks. Furthermore, both religious and nonreligious Sunni Muslims intensely resented the ascendancy of military officers from the Alawite minority sect. Many devout Muslims considered the Alawites as heretics, not Muslims. Many other Muslims regarded the Alawites, who for the first time in modern Syrian history usurped power in Damascus, as socially and culturally inferior.

Consequently, public protests, strikes, demonstrations, and riots organized by the Muslim Brothers erupted in major Syrian cities, notably in the years of 1964, 1965, 1967, and 1969, in reaction to the policies of the "ungodly Ba'th" government. All these eruptions were put down with an iron fist, involving shelling of the central Hama mosque, as well as killing and arresting many hundreds of Muslims.

Upon seizing power in Damascus, Asad, the nondoctrinaire, pragmatic leader, seriously attempted to improve relations with the Sunni Muslim majority population, including the nonmilitant religious sections. To settle the grievances of the Muslim old middle-class he reduced the former harsh socialist measures and encouraged privately owned, small- and medium-size business, industry, and land ownership. To appease the antagonism of many devout Muslims, Asad abolished the former restrictions on religious institutions, allowing the construction of new mosques, and promoted many Muslim clerics in rank. He even declared himself as a devout Muslim, confirmed as such by a religious opinion of the Grand Mufti of Syria, Sheik Ahmad Kaftaru. He also tried to present his fellow Alawites as Shi'te Muslims, not heretics. This by securing another religious opinion from the

Chief Shi'te Imam of Lebanon, Musa al-Sadr, and the Lebanese Grand Mufti Abd al-Amir Qablan.

Yet all these gestures and actions did not change the hostile attitudes of the militant wings of the Muslim Brothers, which remained under strict surveillance by the secret services. During February–May 1973, they organized a series of violent riots in Syrian cities against Asad, the "enemy of Allah." They called for a holy war (Jihad) against his "atheist" and corrupt regime, and the Alawi domination of the army and state. The initial cause and timing of this Muslim eruption was Asad's decision to omit the Islamic Clause from the permanent constitution draft.

This paragraph had initially read that the head of the Syrian state must be a Muslim (in 1950 the Muslim Brothers originally demanded that the constitution assert that Islam was the state religion). This clause had already been omitted by the Marxist-secular Ba'th government in the 1969 provisional constitution. Eventually, following the 1973 riots, which were brutally quelled, Asad decided to reinstate this Islamic paragraph in the permanent constitution.

Still, the Muslim militants would not forsake their struggle against Asad's regime. They made systematic preparations — training abroad and accumulating arms — to start urban guerrilla warfare against the regime for the first time. The pretext and timing was provided by the 1975–76 civil war in Lebanon, leading to Syrian military intervention on the side of the Christian Maronites and against the Muslim Lebanese-Palestinian alliance (see below). Drawing on Muslim popular support as well as the worsening of the economic conditions in Syria, the well-armed Mujahiddin, starting in 1977, launched a long series of guerrilla attacks against government, Ba'thist, and military installations, assassinating state officials, army officers, and Alawite personalities and Soviet experts alike.

In June 1979 for example, they stormed the military artillery college in Aleppo, killing sixty cadets, mostly Alawites. A year later, in June 1980, they made an unsuccessful attempt to kill Asad himself. Around that time the Muslim Brothers established a new "Islamic Front" composed also of nonreligious Sunni professionals, intellectuals, and of other sections of the Syrian middle class. The "Front" issued leaflets blaming Asad and the Ba'th Party for suppressing freedom, the political parties, and the press, as well as distorting democracy and promoting sectarianism.

Challenged by a dangerous urban guerrilla war and a widespread popular uprising, Asad adopted harsh measures against the rebels, including executions, torture, demolition of buildings, and massive arrests. But the Mujahiddin did not give up their rebellion and in early 1982, they stormed the government and party headquarters in the city of Hama, killed many officials, and occupied the city.

In reaction, on February 2, 1982, the city was heavily and indiscriminately shelled by the Syrian army; between 20,000 and 30,000 people were killed—men, women, and children; many people were wounded while many buildings, including mosques and churches, were demolished.

Consequently, the uprising was crushed, Muslim Brothers' activists fled, thousands of Muslims emigrated while many Syrians—angry and fearful—learned this brutal lesson and were resigned to their fate. Asad also learned his lesson, namely to avoid antagonizing Islam and Muslims, embrace them and co-opt them into Syrian public life. Since the early 1990s, while continuing his tight supervision of the militant wing of the Brothers, he granted amnesty to thousands of Brothers in Syria and abroad, releasing many from jail, while allowing moderate Muslim leaders to be elected to the parliament.

He also lifted most restrictions on Islamic publications and dress, opened Koranic schools, built new mosques; all this in order to promote a moderate cultural Islam instead of a militant political one. Possibly to demonstrate his pro-Islamic tendencies, Asad inter alia, enhanced his alliance with the Islamic republics of Iran (Shi'is) and Sudan (Sunnite), as well as backed Muslim guerrilla/terror organizations such as the Lebanese Hezbollah, Palestinian Hamas, and Islamic Jihad.

It would thus appear that Asad, unlike his Ba'thist predecessors, attempted since the 1990s to add an Islamic cultural supplement to the set of tenets that were essential to molding a new national community in Syria. These notions—Pan-Arab nationalism, Syrian patriotism, Ba'thist socialism, anti-imperialism, and anti-Zionism—had been disseminated for years among the public, notably in the educational system.

As a member of the Alawite minority sect, Asad was particularly motivated to stress his adherence to Pan-Arabism, anti-Zionism, and anti-imperialism, in order to gain public legitimacy. But, despite his ideological rhetoric, in his regional and global policies Asad adopted a nonideological pragmatic approach deriving from his personal ambition to survive and advance Syrian national interests.

REGIONAL AND GLOBAL POLICIES

For generations Damascus has prided itself as the hotbed of Pan-Arabism and as a would-be leader of Arab unity, as well as a pioneer of anti-Zionist, anti-Israeli campaigns. In actuality however, Syria was unable to implement the ideas of Arab unity and to lead the Arabs to the elimination of Israel. Syria was weaker than most of its neighbors, not only militarily, but also politically, economically, and even culturally.

It became rather an object of intervention and expansion of other Arab states, and was largely subject to Israeli (and Turkish) military threats. Thus, in the 1940s Syria was a target of Hashemite unity/expansionist schemes: The Greater Syria plan of Transjordan's King Abdallah, and the "Fertile Crescent" design (Iraq, Syria, Lebanon, Palestine, and Transjordan) of the Hashemite monarchy in Baghdad. In the mid-1950s Syria was besieged and menaced by Iraq and Turkey, members of the Baghdad Pact, while in the late 1950s, it was practically incorporated and dominated by Egypt during the UAR period of 1958–61.

Simultaneously, Syria was unable to militarily match Israel in the 1948 all-Arab war against the newly born Jewish state, and later on Damascus was periodically engaged in violent border hostilities with Israel, suffering significant blows despite its topographical advantage in holding the Golan Heights. This strategic inferiority induced Syria to seek Soviet military and economic support, which in turn made Damascus a target of American antagonism and subversion.

Syrian-Soviet ties were greatly enhanced during the Ba'th and neo-Ba'th eras, involving massive Soviet military and economic assistance as well as political and ideological convergences between communist Moscow and socialist-Marxist Damascus. Simultaneously, Syrian-American relations further deteriorated as Washington abandoned its military embargo on Israel and, during the administration of President Kennedy (1961–63), started to supply Israel for the first time with heavy and sophisticated weapons.

America also increased its economic assistance to Israel and continued (particularly during President Johnson's administration, 1963–69) to back Israel in its dispute with Syria over the diversion of the Jordan River waters. To be sure, this Syrian-Israeli dispute, which had already started in the mid-1950s, was the major cause for the June 1967 war. The militant Ba'th and neo-Ba'th regime in Damascus tried to abort Israel's water project by starting works in early 1965 to divert the main tributary of the Jordan River, the Banyas, in the Golan Heights. Syria also em-

ployed the newly established Fatah—a Palestinian guerrilla/ter-
rorist group—to sabotage the Israeli Jordan-Negev water supply
route. Around the same time an internal Ba'th Party circular
stated:

> . . . as regards Palestine, we aim at its liberation from
> conquering Zionism, the annihilation of the State of
> Israel and the return of the Palestinian Arab people
> to their Fatherland . . .

Preparing a war of liberation against Israel, Damascus also endeavored to enlist Cairo's help to prevent Israel by force from
carrying out its water project. Since Nasser rejected the Syrian
call, because his army was not ready for war, he was publicly
accused by a senior Ba'thist leader of "collaborating with the U.S.
in an attempt to secure the peaceful implementation of the Israeli
project."[14]

Subsequently, however, Nasser changed his position and on
May 14, 1967, he dispatched his troops to the demilitarized Sinai
in order "to take a firm stand against the Israeli military threats
and intervene immediately in case of any aggressive action taken
by Israel against Syria."[15]

Israel for its part certainly was not idle; it did use military
power, including its air force, to bomb the Syrian diversion site
as well as to attack Syrian military border positions and shoot
down not a few Syrian combat planes. Yitzhak Rabin, the Israeli
Defense Force (IDF) chief of staff also issued two warnings (in
May 1966 and again a year later in May 1967) against Syria, which
were interpreted by Damascus, Cairo, and Moscow as intended
to topple the Syrian regime by force. Moscow indeed accused
Israel in May 1967 of massing its troops along the Syrian border
with the purpose of overthrowing the Syrian government.

Like Moscow, Washington (for different reasons) had not

been interested at that juncture in an Arab-Israeli war, and similar to Moscow (which indirectly contributed to the war eruption through its misinformation-propaganda campaign), Washington was somewhat involved too. In early June 1967, "the light from Washington shifted from red to yellow. It never turned green; but yellow was enough for the Israelis to know that they could take action without worrying about Washington's reaction."[16]

Israel ended up occupying the Golan Heights (as well as Egyptian Sinai, the Gaza Strip, and the Jordanian-held West Bank) during the Six Day War of 1967, further advancing its military relations with the United States. Syria by contrast, broke off diplomatic relations with the United States and obtained more modern weapons from the USSR, which broke off diplomatic relations with Israel during the war.

Subsequent to the war, which lasted from June 5 to June 11, 1967, Damascus also rejected outright two peace proposals in which Washington was involved:

1. An Israeli peace proposal of June 19, 1967, transmitted through the United States, suggesting Israeli withdrawal from the Golan Heights to the Israeli-Syrian international border, in return for peace, along with demilitarization of the Golan Heights, and a guarantee for free water flow from the Banyas River.
2. An American-British sponsored UN Security Council resolution (242) of November 22, calling for the withdrawal of Israeli troops from territories occupied in the war in return for peaceful co-existence among the states in the region.

Asad, as we know, took a major part in the actions (and in earning blame) in the 1967 Six Day War as Syria's defense minister and air force commander. But after the war, Asad objected to Jadid's strategy of combating Israel by means of a "popular liberation war," in other words, via guerrilla warfare. He preferred to fight Israel through a regular military campaign with the participation of Arab regular armies, regardless of the political-ideological nature of the other participating Arab regimes.

In contrast to Jadid, upon his ascendancy in November 1970, Asad at once accepted Egyptian president Anwar Sadat's offer to join a federation of Arab republics with Egypt and Libya. This federation in Asad's words was to be a stage toward a comprehensive Arab union designed to face the "aggressive and racist Zionist entity," liberate the Arab territories occupied in the 1967 war, and recover all of Palestine.

Subsequently, in early 1971 Asad joined Sadat in secretly planning the 1973 war against Israel, while securing huge quantities of modern weapons from Moscow. Thus on the eve of the October 1973 war, Syria had 2,000 Soviet tanks and 330 combat planes (compared to 430 tanks and 150 planes in 1968). Yet at the same time, Asad refused to continue Syria's ideological links with Moscow, having also resented the political dependence of Syria on the Soviet Union during Jadid's rule. He insisted that Damascus-Moscow relations should be as those between two strategic, political allies.

Contrary to Jadid's approach, before the war Asad enlisted military help from the rival Ba'th regime in Iraq (more than two armored divisions), as well as strategic coordination with Christian-run Lebanon. He also tried to induce King Hussein of Jordan to participate in the 1973 war, but was turned down with a mere promise to dispatch some Jordanian troops to fight Israel in the Golan Heights. Syria and Egypt indeed defeated the Israeli army at the first stage of the war, while Syrian troops succeeded in recapturing the entire Golan Heights. After more fierce and bloody combat, the Israeli Defense Forces, equipped with fresh

U.S. weapons, were able to drive the Syrian and Egyptian troops back and occupy more parts of Syrian and Egyptian land—deploying 45 miles from Damascus and 70 miles from Cairo.

For about a week during the last phase of the war, the Syrians fought back the Israeli troops, with no parallel military actions in the Sinai by the Egyptians. This occurred because President Sadat, with Soviet inducement, requested a ceasefire with Israel without any coordination with Asad. U.S. secretary of state Kissinger (serving under President Nixon), took an active part in helping the Soviet attempts to achieve an Egyptian-Israeli ceasefire. But for a few days he held up Soviet proposals for a Syrian-Israeli truce in order to help Israel's counteroffensive against Syria. Subsequently, Kissinger endeavored in January 1974 to achieve a disengagement of forces agreement between Egypt and Israel, but not between Syria and Israel. This was in line with his step-by-step strategy aiming first at reaching an Egyptian-Israeli settlement.

Syria was initially left behind also because of its militant position. Nevertheless, abandoned (or "betrayed") by Sadat, Asad reluctantly and conditionally accepted an October 23, 1973, UN Security Council resolution 338 which called for a ceasefire and the implementation of the 1967 UN resolution 242.

Six months later, on May 31, he also signed a disengagement agreement with Israel, following active mediation efforts by Kissinger, with no Soviet participation. Indeed, and highly significantly at that juncture, the realistic and seasoned Syrian leader presumably reached two new and important conclusions:

1. That Syria (and the Arab world) was unable to destroy Israel by force; hence it should aim primarily at regaining its own occupied territories—the Golan Heights—through political negotiations and agreements with Israel, plus a political settlement of the Palestinian issue.

2. These political processes must be carried indirectly under American sponsorship, since only Washington can induce Israel to return the occupied Golan Heights. While maintaining the strategic military alliance with Moscow to enhance Syrian security and deterrence, Damascus should maneuver between the two superpowers as well as endeavor to push a wedge between the United States and Israel.

As Asad stated to a Ba'th convention in 1975:

> . . . we are in the midst of the battle and the road is long, and we have to prepare ourselves militarily and act politically and economically to strengthen the military action . . . among our important and main weapons are . . . Arab solidarity, Arab unity. . . . We have made efforts to establish positive relations . . . with the U.S. . . . to gain its friendship in order to turn its power into a neutral one, and to weaken this power's support to our direct enemy . . . [17]

The previous year in mid-June 1974, Asad welcomed President Nixon on the first visit of an American president to Damascus. Damascus and Washington then resumed diplomatic relations, the United States promised financial aid to Syria, while Asad hailed the important role of the United States in the region and remarked that he "was not a Soviet puppet." But Asad soon became disappointed by U.S. policies, particularly those during President Ford's administration that substantially increased its financial and military aid to Israel. While siding more with Israel on the Golan dispute, Kissinger, who continued to serve as secretary of state, also insisted on carrying on his step-by-step strategy. He refused to link Israel's withdrawal in Sinai within an Egyptian-Israeli agreement to an Israeli withdrawal on the Golan Heights as part of a comprehensive Arab-Israeli settlement. Asad even announced on various occasions (mostly to American media) his readiness to make peace with Israel (in fact a nonbelligerency agreement without diplomatic and economic relations) in return for the Golan Heights as well as the settlement of the Palestinian problem. Simultaneously, in April 1976 Asad concluded with Yitzhak Rabin, Israel's new prime minister, a secret agreement under American auspices, to practically divide Lebanon into two spheres of influence: Syrian in the north and center and Israeli in the south.

Syria had succeeded previously in obtaining American approval for its intervention in Lebanon's civil war on the side of the Christian-Maronite government. Furthermore, Asad developed high expectations regarding the newly elected U.S. president, Jimmy Carter, who similar to Asad advocated a comprehensive settlement for the Arab-Israeli conflict, including a "homeland" for the Palestinian people. Indeed, Carter met Asad for the first time in Geneva in May 1977 and was deeply impressed with Asad's personality, although not with his extreme anti-Israeli position.

Nevertheless, after coordinating with Moscow, a U.S.-USSR joint communiqué was issued on October 1, 1977, calling for a comprehensive settlement of the Arab-Israeli conflict in the framework of the Geneva Conference (which had initially convened after the October 1973 war and was boycotted then by Syria). This initiative, which was in line with the Syrian position, threatened to undermine the secret, Egyptian-Israeli talks regarding peace between the two countries. Both Egypt and Israel were concerned, lest the Geneva Conference would grant Syria and the USSR a veto power over a separate Egyptian-Israeli accord. Subsequently however, Carter was persuaded by Israel and its supporters in Washington to drop the Geneva Conference in favor of a separate Egyptian-Israeli deal. Thus, following Sadat's historic visit to Israel in November 1977, the Camp David Accords (September 1978) and the Egyptian-Israeli Peace Treaty (March

1979) were signed under American auspices. Asad found himself let down, if not betrayed by the United States. This global strategic failure was one of the main reasons for Asad's decision to sign a friendship and cooperation agreement with the Soviet Union for the first time in October 1980. The other main reason for this tightening of relations with Moscow was Asad's failure to forge a regional Arab bloc vis-à-vis Israel.

REGIONAL ALLIES? IRAQ, JORDAN, AND THE PLO

Since 1974, after the first Egyptian disengagement agreement with Israel, Asad sought to create an alternative Pan-Arab alliance to the Egyptian-Syrian axis. Neighboring Iraq was his prior choice owing to its unique combination of military and economic power, which could provide strategic depth for Syria, as well as its Ba'thist regime's ideology of Arab unity and anti-Zionism. But Baghdad, which had contributed a large military force to help Syria in the 1973 war, resented Damascus's acceptance of UN Security Council resolution 338, interpreting it as a Syrian recognition of Israel. Iraq insisted that Syria should withdraw its recognition of this resolution as a condition for starting unity negotiations with Damascus. Asad refused, and the two Ba'thist regimes exchanged accusations and insults.

Following the Camp David Accords, Iraqi president Ahmad Hasan al-Bakr suggested that Baghdad and Damascus join forces against the Egyptian-Israeli accord. By late October 1978, Asad and Bakr signed a charter in Baghdad for "Joint National Action" which provided for the "closest form of unity ties" including "complete military unity" as well as "economic, political, and cultural unification." It depicted this "historical Pan-Arab step" as a serious search "for a greater strength in confronting the present Zionist onslaught against the Arab nation."[18] But after Saddam

Hussein assumed power in Baghdad (officially he succeeded Bakr as president in July 1979) the unity talks encountered major difficulties. Asad rejected Saddam's demands for a full merger between Iraq and Syria and for immediate deployment of Iraqi troops in Syria. Asad advocated a step-by-step approach, possibly fearing Iraqi domination.

Consequently the talks were suspended by Iraq, mutual accusations followed, and the two states expelled their respective ambassadors in 1980. When the Iran-Iraq war started the same year, Damascus sided with Tehran against Baghdad, while Syrian-Iraqi relations sank to their lowest levels since their respective independence.

Alongside his attempts to enlist Iraq's cooperation, Asad made special efforts to create a "Greater Syria" strategic alliance with Lebanon, Jordan, and the Palestinians. This alliance under his leadership could become a new regional power vis-à-vis Iraq, Egypt, and Israel.

Jordan was the most important strategic component in this potential alliance, because of its long border with Israel and its well-trained army. In April 1975, Asad suggested to King Hussein the creation of a Joint Supreme Leadership Council to prepare the integration of the two states in the political, military, economic, and cultural fields. Having been isolated in the Arab world following the Rabat Conference of October 1974, Hussein accepted Asad's offer.

Subsequently, a series of steps were taken by the two countries to move toward full integration. But, by late 1977 Hussein changed his mind, or tactics, in view of improved Syrian relations with Jordan's enemy, the PLO, and Asad's militant attitude toward an Egyptian-Israeli peace. Although Hussein was displeased that he had not been consulted regarding Sadat's initiative, he did not want to alienate either Egypt, the major Arab State, or Israel, Jordan's tacit strategic ally. King Hussein also was forced by late 1979 into choosing between Saddam Hussein and Hafiz Asad. He preferred Saddam for strategic and economic reasons.

This prompted Asad to apply military and diplomatic pressure on Jordan in 1980, and to employ his agents to terrorize or assassinate Jordanian officials, while calling for the overthrow of King Hussein and the Hashemite monarchy. Since King Hussein would not be intimidated, in 1985 Asad renewed his terrorist campaign against Jordanian targets (not surprisingly, Syrian-Jordanian relations would largely recover only after the deaths, fifteen years later, of both Arab rulers—King Hussein in 1999 and Hafiz Asad in 2000). With King Hussein's ultimate refusal to integrate into Asad's Greater Syria strategy, the remaining potential parties were Lebanon and the Palestinians.

Lebanon had been historically and ideologically considered by Damascus as the western part of Syria. While Damascus has never opened an embassy in Beirut, Lebanon was important to Syria economically (for trade, banking, and Syrian laborers), politically (owing to its ties with the United States and Europe), and strategically (because of its southern border with Israel).

The Palestinians were valuable to Asad—ideologically and politically—as a major issue of Pan-Arab nationalism and anti-Zionism; Palestine also having been considered part of southern Syria. As we know, the Ba'th and neo-Ba'th regimes had extended military, logistic, and diplomatic assistance to the Palestinian armed organizations, initially Fatah and later the PLO, in their struggles against Israel. In October 1974, Asad was a leading supporter of the Rabat Conference's decision to recognize the PLO as the sole representative of the Palestinian people, and in March 1975 he offered Yasser Arafat, who had moved his headquarters from Jordan to Lebanon, to form a joint Syrian-PLO political and military command.

But, when the Lebanese civil war erupted several weeks later, Asad was forced to choose between the two warring factions: the

conservative Christian Maronites or the radical PLO–Lebanese
Muslim alliance. Contrary to the Ba'thist ideological tenets, Asad
backed—with Syrian military force—the weak Maronite-led government, calculating that this could facilitate his strategic design
to control Lebanon. As a result, his troops fought against the
strong PLO-Muslim alliance, because this alliance was likely to
take over Lebanon and pose a more cohesive radical challenge to
Asad's design. Yet, Asad explained his stance in the anti–PLO-
Muslim campaign with the following words:

> A decisive military action [by the radical axis] would
> open doors to every foreign intervention, particularly
> Israel's intervention. Let us all visualize . . . if Israel
> were to intervene and save [Christian] Arabs from
> [Muslim] Arabs.

To Arafat, Asad said:

> You do not represent Palestine more than we do.
> There is neither a Palestinian people nor a Palestinian
> entity, there is only Syria . . . and Palestine is an in-
> separable part of Syria.[19]

Significantly, Asad obtained American backing for his pro-
Maronite, anti-PLO campaign, while rejecting Soviet requests to
stop his military offensive against the PLO-Muslim alliance. But,
during 1977, Asad changed his own alliances in Lebanon, as
Maronite Christian militias—encouraged by the new right-wing
Israeli government—forcibly resisted the continued Syrian control over Lebanon. To counterbalance these militias and reinstate
his Pan-Arab image, following Sadat's visit to Israel Asad renewed his close ties with the PLO and the Lebanese Muslim Left.
He now needed this radical backing vis-à-vis the hostile attitude

toward Damascus by the new Israeli government, partly provoked by Christian Maronites.

In December 1981, Israel formally annexed the Golan Heights,
drawing American anger; and in June 1982, the Israeli army invaded southern Lebanon, ostensibly to destroy the PLO infrastructure. In fact however, Defense Minister Ariel Sharon who
had masterminded this campaign, strove to achieve two more
goals: to oust the Syrian army from Lebanon and to install a pro-
Israel Maronite government in Beirut.

The U.S. administration of President Ronald Reagan, which
initially disapproved of the Israeli invasion, supported the May
1983 political agreement between Beirut and Jerusalem. Washington also sent U.S. navy ships and marines to uphold the
new Lebanese-Maronite government. So did France. Convinced
that the Reagan administration was hostile to him, Asad depicted the 1983 agreement as "worse than the Camp David Accords . . . [it is] part of the American-Zionist plan to dominate
[our region]." Previously, he reacted similarly to the 1981 strategic cooperation agreement between America and Israel saying: "[it] directly puts U.S. forces against us."[20] Apparently
upon his directive, the Lebanese militant Shi'is group Hezbollah carried out a series of suicide attacks against American,
French, and Israeli targets in Lebanon. On April 18, 1983, for
example, the American embassy in Beirut was demolished by a
suicide car-bomb killing 63 people; and later on October 23
American and French military barracks were similarly destroyed
by Shi'is suicide squads, claiming the lives of 241 American marines and 58 French soldiers.

Many more attacks were carried out against Israeli military
targets causing great loss of life. Consequently, the United States
and France withdrew their units from Beirut while the new Lebanese president Amin Jumayyil, under Syrian pressure, abrogated
the Lebanese-Israeli agreement of May 1983.

Early in 1985 Israel pulled its troops from most of Lebanon. Syria then gradually extended its control over Lebanon by means of manipulation, intimidation, and assassination; and ultimately Damascus formalized its indirect domination of Lebanon through the 1989 Ta'if Agreement. Thus, Damascus emerged victorious in its struggle with Jerusalem over Lebanon. But gaining control in Lebanon remained the only Syrian achievement in its global and regional strategies.

Although Washington acknowledged Syrian control and domination over Lebanon, it strongly condemned Damascus's involvement in international terrorism, particularly against Israeli targets, placing it on a U.S. State Department "blacklist." The Soviet Union apparently did not activate the 1980 Syrian-Soviet "friendship and cooperation agreement" with Damascus when it refrained from helping Asad vis-à-vis the Israeli offensive in 1982. Following the ascendancy of Soviet leader Mikhail Gorbachev in 1985 the Soviet Union substantially decreased its military and economic aid to Syria.

Regional friction was rampant throughout the Middle East. Damascus further alienated Yasser Arafat by failing to defend his guerrillas in the 1982 war and expelling him from Damascus in 1983. King Hussein of Jordan deeply resented Syrian military pressures and terrorism, while Saddam Hussein of Iraq endeavored to destabilize Asad's rule because of Syria's continued support of Iran in its bloody war with Baghdad, which lasted from 1980–88, and beyond.

STRATEGIC ALLIANCE WITH IRAN VS. STRATEGIC BALANCE WITH ISRAEL

To be sure, Asad vehemently objected to the Iraqi invasion of Iran as a wrong war and: "[a] waste of Arab potential . . . in the confrontation against Israel [which] created a new enemy for the

Arab nations [in Iran,] . . . on the same level as Israel," instead of considering the Iranian Islamic revolutionary regime as a potential crucial ally to Arab peoples. Asad went on to say:

> This revolution introduced important changes in the strategic balance . . . from regional and global points of view; [it] supports the Arabs without hesitation, in action for the sake of liberating our lands. How can we be allowed to lose a great achievement and lose a country like Iran of the Islamic revolution . . . with all its human, military, and economic potential?[21]

Indeed, during the devastating Iraq-Iran war, Asad supported Iran logistically and diplomatically while providing facilities for Iran's air force at Syrian airports. He did this against the ideological notions of both Arabism and Ba'thism—that is cooperating with a non-Arab, non-Sunni, militant, Islamic regime in a bloody war against a sister Arab state with a Ba'thist regime. Asad embarked on this bold policy not only because of Ba'thist conceptual, personal, and Arab regional rivalry with Saddam Hussein, but because Asad was deeply concerned about the Syrian strategic balance with Israel. His goal was, in part, to prepare a coordinated military offensive under suitable global and regional circumstances. No less important was to deter Israel from attacking Syria and to negotiate a political settlement with it from a position of military strength. Asad had indeed been obsessed by the need to achieve a balance of power with Israel even before seizing power in Damascus.

Asad viewed this strategic balance in military, economic, and political Pan-Arab terms, namely Inter-Arab cooperation, based on a coherent Egyptian-Syrian military axis. But following Sadat's "defection," and the failure to build an alternative alliance with Iraq, Asad developed in the late 1970s–early 1980s a new strategy:

to achieve for Syria a military parity with Israel with massive Soviet help, but without relying on other Arab regimes.

Simultaneously, he intended to cooperate with Iran in toppling Saddam Hussein's regime, and making Iraq a component in a new strategic axis: Tehran, Baghdad, Damascus, and Beirut. As it happened, by 1988, Asad was unable to achieve these strategic goals. The Iraq-Iran war ended with a certain advantage to Saddam's Iraq. In addition to supplying oil cheaply, Iran could only help Syria to arm and finance the Hezbollah militants in their guerrilla warfare along the Lebanese-Israeli border.

The Soviet Union under Gorbachev dramatically changed its policy toward the Syrian quest for strategic balance with Israel. Gorbachev urged Asad, since 1987, to seek a political settlement with Israel based on balance of interests. While allowing Jewish immigration to Israel for the first time, Moscow also reduced the supply of weapons to Damascus and withdrew about 3,000 (out of 6,000) Soviet experts and demanded Damascus to now pay hard currency for Soviet arms. This demand seriously compounded the acute economic crisis, which Syria had undergone in previous years, mainly owing to its huge military expenditures (65 percent of its annual budget).

Consequently, Asad was induced again to substantially change his global and regional strategy—i.e., to seek rapprochement with the United States, the major superpower, and with Egypt, the major regional Arab power; this in order to improve his political position and gain diplomatic backing in his conflict with Israel.

RAPPROCHEMENT WITH THE UNITED STATES AND PEACE TALKS WITH ISRAEL

Encouraged by the fact that George Bush Sr. had been elected to the U.S. presidency without the support of the American-Jewish vote, Asad stated early in 1989:

> [The United States] as a superpower directly respon-
> sible for international security and peace should give
> up its Zionist point of view, put an end to the Zionist
> danger . . . force the Zionist enemy to withdraw from
> the occupied territories and execute the international
> decisions to achieve just and true and comprehensive
> peace in the region.[22]

President Bush and Secretary of State Baker were indeed critical of continued Israeli occupation of Syrian and Palestinian territories. They were inclined to initiate a new "framework for
action and cooperation with Syria" toward a political settlement
of the conflict with Israel.

As it happened, Asad's archenemy, Saddam Hussein, indirectly
(and ironically) helped Damascus to gain a "breakthrough" in its
relations with Washington. Iraq's invasion of Kuwait in August
of 1990 provided Asad with a rare opportunity to help Bush and
be rewarded accordingly. To this end Asad was ready again to
compromise his Pan-Arab Ba'thist ideology and dispatch Syrian
troops to join the American-led military coalition, which ousted
the Iraqi army from Kuwait. Asad's gains were substantial: his
enemy Saddam was dealt as serious military defeat, he obtained
large financial grants from the Arab Gulf states, and he was able
to oust the Maronite independent leader General Awn from Beirut by brutal force. Asad thus completed his control over Lebanon with tacit American approval, and following a Bush-Asad
summit in Geneva in March of 1990 and the end of the war one
year later, Asad expressed new optimism regarding the American
position on the Syrian-Israeli conflict, saying:

> The current [American] administration is seriously
> oriented toward pushing the peace process forward.
> This seriousness has never been felt by us before. . . .

The United States has not recognized the Israeli annexation of the Golan. It rejected this annexation.[23]

Yet, Asad was now ready to accept the Bush-Baker proposal
for a Madrid peace conference in October 1991: a regional (not
global) peace conference under American and Soviet auspices
(not the UN) and for the first time direct negotiations with Israel
on the basis of UN Security Council resolutions 242 and 338.
Israel's new and inflexible prime minister, Yitzhak Shamir, accepted President Bush's invitation to Madrid only after heavy
American pressure.

During the first phase of negotiations—mostly in Washington,
D.C.—Israel and Syria made little progress. Only after the Israeli
elections of June 1992, which installed the Labor Party's Yitzhak
Rabin as prime minister did the Israeli, and subsequently Syrian,
positions become more flexible inter alia in anticipation of the
November 1992 U.S. elections. Syria initially was concerned
about the pro-Israeli positions of newly elected president Clinton.
Damascus was also unhappy with U.S. support of and involvement in the Israeli-PLO Oslo Accords, which occurred in September 1993, and also that Arafat signed these accords without
previous coordination with Damascus. But when they met for
the first time in Geneva in January 1994, Clinton was convinced
that Asad truly agreed to have normal relations with Israel and
that "Syria is the key to the achievement of an enduring and
comprehensive peace."[24] He urged Rabin to adopt crucial decisions regarding Israel's withdrawal from the Golan Heights.
Washington continued to be actively involved in the Damascus-
Jerusalem negotiations, providing its own blueprint for a settlement, while balancing between the attempts of both Rabin and
Asad to win its backing.

Clinton tended to side more with Rabin, while also taking
under his auspices the May 1994 peace treaty between Israel and

Jordan, which undermined Syrian demands, namely that Israel should withdraw to the ceasefire line of June 4, 1967, and not to the international boundary, as was the case in the Israeli-Jordanian settlement. Asad kept insisting on his position then and again during his second meeting with Clinton in Damascus in October 1994. Repeating his commitment to normal peace relations with Israel, Asad suggested that American satellites should supervise the demilitarized areas in the Golan, following a peace agreement, and objected to Israeli early warning stations on the Golan.

Syrian-Israeli peace negotiations continued after the assassination of Prime Minister Rabin in November 1995, and during the terms of Peres, Netanyahu, and Barak, serving successively as Israeli prime ministers. Both Syrian and Israeli leaders used various tactics to influence the positions of one another. Asad for example, would occasionally unleash the Hezbollah to hit Israeli targets, as well as direct his media to verbally attack Israel. But he also made positive gestures toward Israel, such as allowing Syrian Jews to emigrate, and permitting Israeli-Arab citizens to visit Syria. For its part, Israel would retaliate against Hezbollah targets, killing innocent civilians as well. In May 2000, however, Israel's prime minister, Ehud Barak, made a significant step toward omitting the "Hezbollah card" from Asad's hand, by withdrawing the IDF from Israel's Security Zone to the international boundary. This was a last attempt to sway Asad toward a peace agreement with Israel. But this was too late, as Asad died on June 10, 2000, after rejecting Barak's final offer regarding Israeli-Syrian peace in March 2000. Transmitted to Asad by Clinton at Lake Geneva, Barak suggested full Israeli withdrawal from the Golan Heights, down to Lake Tiberias, but with no Syrian access to the lake.

This offer fell short of Asad's demand to return to the June 4, 1967, ceasefire line, touching the northeastern tip of the lake for several kilometers. Neither Asad nor Barak would accept a compromise solution, i.e., to turn the disputed strip of land—several kilometers long and 200 meters wide—into a joint tourist area with joint sovereignty or a special status.

BASHAR ASAD IN POWER: QUO VADIS SYRIA?

The chances for a Syrian-Israeli peace have been diminished since the succession to power of Bashar, Hafiz Asad's son. Although stating several times that peace with Israel has remained Syria's strategic option, Bashar has been unable and unwilling to breach his father's legacy regarding the June 4, 1967, line. And to be sure, Israeli prime minister Ariel Sharon (in power since early 2001) as well as the Israeli public, are reluctant to adopt Barak's line even for full peace with Syria. Bashar has partly contributed to this Israeli rejection, by periodically unleashing Hezbollah attacks against Israelis, harboring the militant Hamas and Islamic Jihad, hailing the Palestinian Intifada, and resorting to harsh, anti-Israeli and anti-Jewish rhetoric. For example, in the presence of Pope John Paul II, at the Syrian-Israeli ceasefire line in May 2001, Bashar equated Israel with the Nazis, stated that the Jews killed Jesus, and suggested forming a Muslim-Christian front against Judaism.

Similarly, the prospects for Bashar gaining the younger president Bush's (George W.) support for Syria regarding peace with Israel, have been rather slim since his ascendancy and particularly after the terrorist attacks against the United States on September 11, 2001.

These prospects have been far and away from those during the previous U.S. administrations of presidents George Bush Sr. and Bill Clinton. The latter administration even suggested incorporating Syria into a "dual containment" regional alliance (following a peace agreement with Israel)—vis-à-vis Iran and Iraq. But contrary to this goal, Syria under Bashar strengthened its strategic ties with Iran, and significantly enhanced its new political and economic links with Iraq. Simultaneously, "Damascus may have violated the UN arms embargo against Iraq by transporting weapons and military equipment delivered to Syrian ports into Iraq, via trucks and rail routes" (July 2002). And according to a CIA report (December 2001), "Damascus also continued its efforts to assemble—probably with considerable North Korean assistance—liquid-fueled, SCUD C missiles."[25]

As it were, these Syrian actions, plus Damascus's endeavors to develop weapons of mass destruction—notably chemical and biological—likely would qualify Bashar's Syria to become a member of the "axis of evil," in accordance with the current president Bush's 2002 State of the Union Address. Indeed, by mid-October 2003, the White House rendered its backing to the Syria Accountability Act, 2002, that was approved by the U.S. Congress on October 15, 2003.[26] This act calls on Syria to halt support for terrorism and to end its occupation of Lebanon and stop its development of weapons of mass destruction. If implemented, it would entail imposing diplomatic and economic sanctions against Syria by the United States.

CONCLUSIONS

While analyzing these new American steps, no one must either underestimate or over rate the potential dangers of these Syrian policies or actions. Regarding weapons of mass destruction, there is no evidence that Syria is developing a nuclear capability, as is the case with Iran and North Korea. And unlike Iraq's Saddam, Syrian rulers have never used chemical weapons against their enemies, internal or external, while considering these weapons as a deterrence vis-à-vis Israel's nuclear capability and strategic edge. Also, unlike Saddam who invaded Iran in 1980 and Kuwait in

1990, Asad was "officially invited" in 1976 by the Lebanese government to send his troops to pacify the Lebanese civil war, which had started the previous year. Subsequently, Syria's presence or occupation of Lebanon has continued and has been anchored in the official mutual agreements between Syria and Lebanon of 1989 and 1991. Finally, since the American occupation of Iraq, Damascus has also made some attempts to mend fences with Washington both by word and by deed, notably by helping to hunt down some al-Qaida terrorists within Syria.

Taking into account these recent attempts by Bashar Asad, his domestic regional predicaments, as well as the significant record of Hafiz Asad's cooperation with the United States over many years, Washington should carefully calculate its new strategy with Damascus. An American military attack on Syria, apart from exhausting U.S. military and economic resources and exposing U.S. troops to mounting guerrilla warfare, is also likely to critically damage American interests (oil trade) and image in most Arab and Muslim nations, many of which already consider the United States to be a neo-imperialistic, hostile power.

American economic and diplomatic sanctions against Syria may be effective in certain areas, such as in closing more offices of terrorist organizations in Damascus and withdrawing more Syrian troops from Lebanon, but it is hardly likely that Damascus will yield to American pressure regarding its vital national interests, such as developing a deterrence vis-à-vis Israel and continuing to control Lebanon. Furthermore, Damascus is likely to react to American pressures by strengthening its strategic cooperation with Iran and organizing a regional network of anti-American terrorism, with Shi'is Hezbollah as its model and with the cooperation of militant Shi'is from Iraq and Iran. In addition, simultaneously, Damascus will present itself again, as a major center of Pan-Arab nationalism, since Egypt has "deviated" from "true" Arabism and Iraq has been occupied by the United States.

Damascus may thus become a focus of Arab nationalistic struggle against an American regional presence and interests.

Given these potential grim scenarios, Washington may also consider a different strategy toward Damascus: embracing Syria, and gradually integrating it into a positive brand of "Pax Americana," namely a network of pragmatic Arab regimes, along with Turkey and Israel, that would cooperate with the United States to combat terrorism, maintain stability, and develop their economies. For Syria, this can also entail full peace with Israel in return for the Golan Heights, withdrawing from Lebanon, diminishing relations with Iran, as well as reforming its economy and political system. Bashar is obviously aware of Syria's weaker geo-strategic situation—surrounded by pro-American regimes: Turkey, Israel, Jordan, and Iraq. He does not seek a military confrontation with any of these regimes, certainly not with the United States—which may lead to his demise. Bashar might have incentives to cooperate with the United States provided Washington extends economic aid and investment, erases Syria from the list of countries supporting terrorism, and helps it to regain the Golan Heights.

Damascus is likely to and must render full peace to Israel for the Golan and then it should not need its alliances with Islamic Iran and Lebanon's Hezbollah. Similarly, an agreed settlement of the Israeli-Palestinian conflict should also seal off Damascus's relations with Hamas and Islamic Jihad, although Damascus must immediately stop helping these militant Palestinians as a contribution to combat terrorism.

Concerning economic and political liberalization: since his ascent to power, Bashar has endeavored to modernize the backward and plagued Syrian economy and initially also to allow more political freedoms. He appointed Western-educated economists to senior positions, introduced a modern banking system, the Internet, and cellular phone technology.

Nevertheless, Bashar has a long way to go to reform his economy and needs American help. This is certainly equally relevant to the political system which has continued to be autocratic, devoid of freedoms of assembly, speech, and publication, as well as suppressing human rights. Attentive to the requests of Syrian intellectuals, Bashar initially permitted some freedom of expression in newly formed political clubs and in some newspapers. But under the pressure of the conservative "old guard" from his father's regime, he subsequently suppressed these new signs of freedom.

However, it appears that in the last two years, Bashar managed to weaken the "old guard," appointed his own loyalists to senior positions, and resumed his limited political reforms. For example, he tolerated a newly published petition in May 2003, by many hundreds of Syrian intellectuals, engineers, lawyers, and political activists, calling for the abrogation of martial law, the release of political prisoners, and allowing freedom of opinion and assembly.

Bashar has also introduced certain Ba'th Party changes—providing for elections rather than appointments to party positions, and abolishing party members' advantage in obtaining government appointments. He has also permitted to freely import foreign movies, publish "independent" newspapers, and establish a private university. These reforms are obviously insufficient from the American point of view. But Washington cannot expect Syria—as well as Egypt, Iraq, and Jordan—to embrace Western-style democracy within a short time (or at any time). The United States may accept a Syrian form of "democracy and pluralism" as long as it safeguards human rights and civil liberties. Washington can help Damascus to implement these notions by political persuasion and financial inducements.

Finally, as far as its regional policy is concerned, it is a vested U.S. interest to bring Syria into the fold, in parallel with the Palestinians. Helping Syria and the Palestinians to settle their conflict with Israel is likely to enhance America's position in the Middle East, clean up its tarnished image as a neo-imperialistic crusader power, and help it establish a strategic network of stable, pragmatic (but not fully democratic) Arab regimes, willing to cooperate with the United States to combat terrorism and gradually reform their own systems.

NOTES

1. Respective quotations from Neil MacFarquhar, "Syrian Official Says Relations with U.S. Plunge to New Low," *New York Times*, October 12, 2003, A12; *Al-Hayat*, July 28, 2003; Steven R. Weisman, "U.S. Threatens to Impose Penalties Against Syrians," *New York Times*, April 15, 2003, B3; and Charles V. Pena, "The Real Axis of Evil," April 23, 2003, http://www.cato.org/cgi-bin/scripts/printtech.cgi/dailys/04-23-03.html.
2. *Al-Safir* (Lebanon), March 27, 2003; *New York Times*, April 15, 2003, B3.
3. Adam Zagorin, "Saddam's Syrian Stash," *Time*, October 20, 2003.
4. IMRA, http://www.state.gov/t/us/rm, September 16, 2003.
5. The Economist Intelligence Unit Country Report, November 2002, 14–16.
6. Richard W. Stevenson and Earl Hulse, "Bush Tells Israel It Has the Right to Defend Itself," *New York Times,* October 7, 2003, A1, A13.
7. http://www.msnbc.com/news/904432.asp.
8. Circular, Secret, September 25, 1957, Declassified Documents Quarterly Catalog (Washington, DC: Carrollton Press, 1989) 1544.
9. U.S. Department of State, *Foreign Relations of the United*

States, vol. IX, 1952–1954 (Washington, DC: Government Printing Office, 1986); vol. XIII, 1955–1957 (idem, 1988).

10. Memorandum, American Embassy, Damascus, to U.S. Dept. of State, August 17, 1957, Declassified Documents 71G (1977) .904432.asp.

11. NSC, U.S. Policy, November 4, 1958, Declassified Documents Quarterly Catalog 2566 (1989).

12. Ghalib Kayali, Hafiz al-Asad—"Leader and Message" (in Arabic, Damascus, 1977), 31–33.

13. *New York Times*, October 19 and November 14, 1970.

14. See respectively, Avraham Ben-Tzur, ed., *The Syrian Ba'th Party and Israel*, (Givat Haviva: Center for Arab and Afro-Asian Studies, 1968), 5–8; Itamar Rabinovich, *Syria Under the Ba'th, 1963–1966* (Jerusalem: Israel Universities Press, 1972), 96.

15. *Middle East Record* 1967 (Tel Aviv: The Shiloach Center, Tel Aviv University, 1971), 185.

16. William B. Quandt, "Lyndon Johnson and the June 1967 War," *Middle East Journal*, no. 46 (1992), 199.

17. Statement of the National Leadership of the Ba'th Party, the Ba'th 12th National Congress, Damascus, 1975.

18. Full text in *Journal of Palestine Studies* 8, no. 2 (1979), 200–202.

19. Moshe Ma'oz, *Asad: The Sphinx of Damascus: A Political Biography* (London: Weidenfeld and Nicolson, 1988), 127–29.

20. See respectively, Damascus Radio, March 9, 1981, and August 1, 1983.

21. See respectively, Damascus Radio, November 7, 1980; Mustafa Tlas, ed., *So Said Asad* (in Arabic, Damascus, 1984), 389–90.

22. *Tishrin* (Syria), January 21, 1989.

23. *Washington Post*, July 29, 1991.

24. *Al-Safir* (Lebanon), January 18, 1994.
25. Raymond Tanter, "Classifying Evil: Bush Administration Rhetoric and Policy Toward Rogue Regimes; Policy Focus #44," the Washington Institute for Near East Policy, 2003.
26. Carl Hulse, "Syria: U.S. House Approves Sanctions," *New York Times*, October 16, 2003.

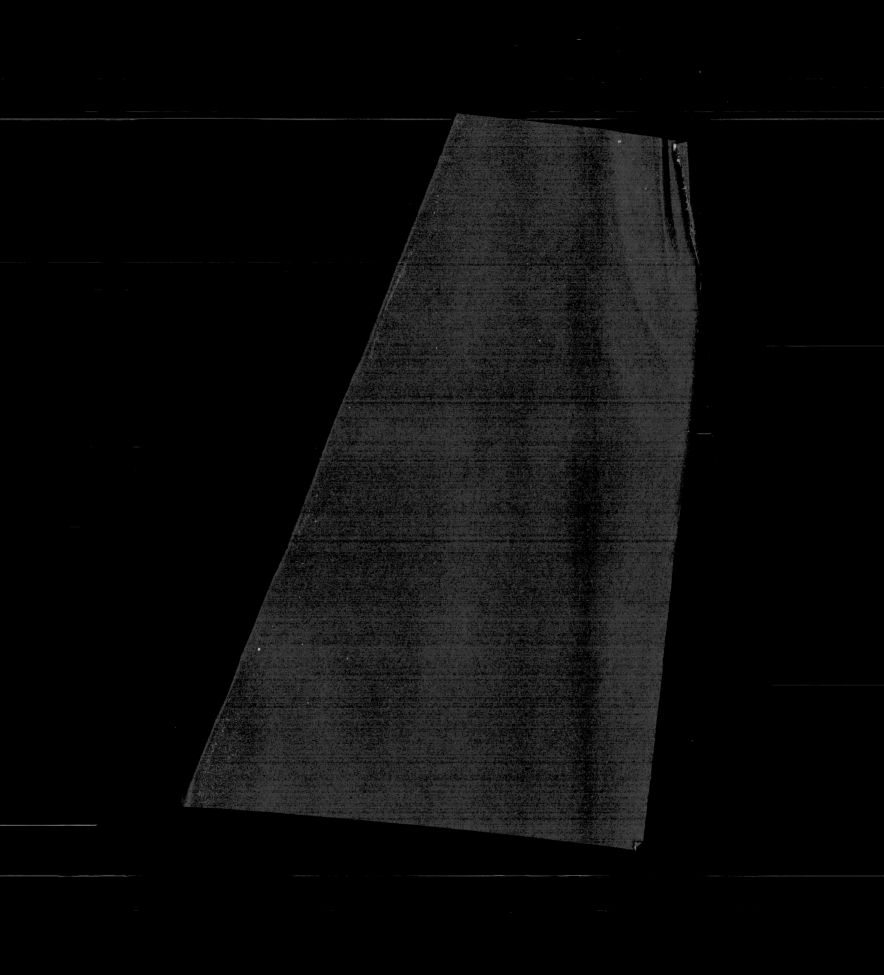

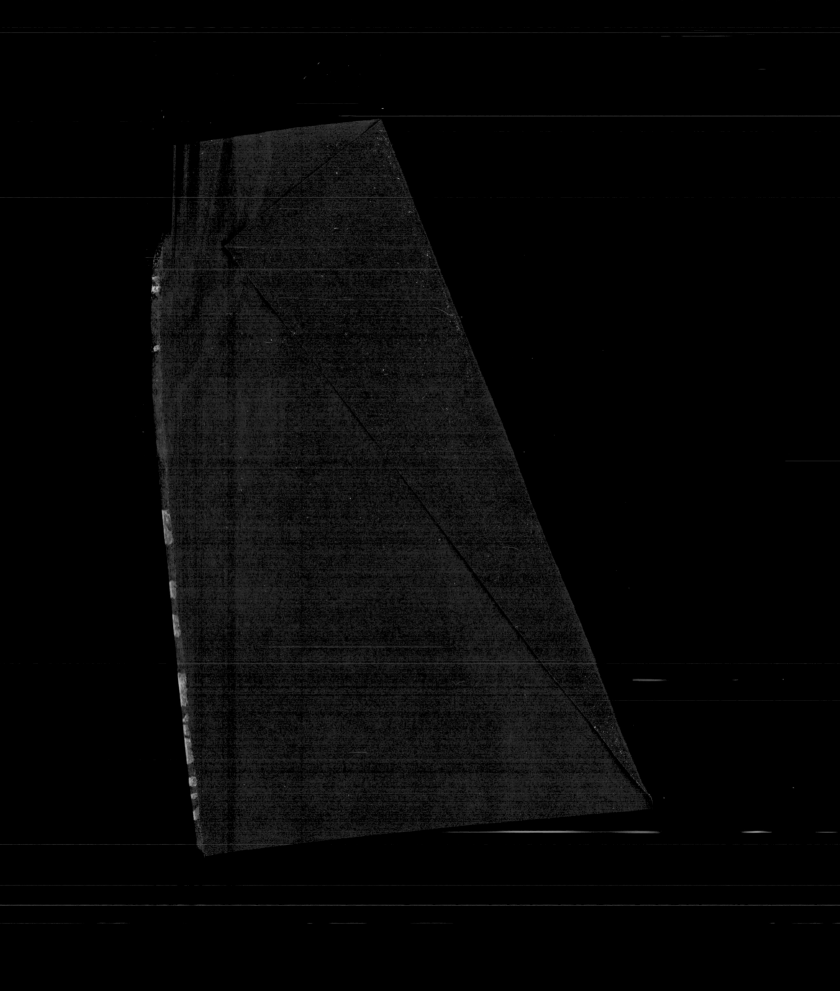